Strange Creatures

ROSIE ANDREWS

authorHOUSE®

AuthorHouse™ UK Ltd.
1663 Liberty Drive
Bloomington, IN 47403 USA
www.authorhouse.co.uk
Phone: 0800.197.4150

Published by AuthorHouse   03/05/2014

ISBN: 978-1-4918-7685-5 (sc)
ISBN: 978-1-4918-7686-2 (hc)
ISBN: 978-1-4918-7687-9 (e)

LIST OF QUOTATIONS

All quotations, unless otherwise stated, are from the Internet as listed below:—

1. Benjamin Franklin—searchquotes.com
2. George Bernard Shaw—goodreads.com
3. Dalai Lama—Brainyquotes.com
4. Marilyn vos Savant—goodreads.com
5. Thomas Alva Edison—thomasaedison.com
6. J Lincoln Fenn—goodreads.com
7. Joan Didion—brainyquotes.com
8. Mark Twain—goodreads.com
9. Robert Neeley Bellah—brainyquotes.com
10. Albert Camus—wikiquote.org
11. Katie Price—brainyquotes.com
12. Russell Brand—brainyquotes.com
13. Dorothy Parker—quotationspage.com
14. Philippians 4 Verse 19 Holy Bible
15. General Omar M. Bradley Armistice Day 1948—opinionbug.com
16. George Santayana—quotationspage.com
17. Erica Jong—from "Fear of Flying"
18. Anon—quoteworld.org
19. Ted Grant—photoquotes.com
20. Dirk Bogarde—brainyquote.com
21. Ansel Adams—photographyabout.com
22. Hannah Harrington—"Saving June"—goodreads.com
23. Satchel Paige—brainyquote.com
24. Judge Judith Sheindlin—searchquotes.com
25. Unknown—Boardofwisdom.com
26. Margaret Mitchell from "Gone with the Wind—goodreads.com
27. Miles Kington—goodreads.com
28. Kate Moss—brainyquotes.com
29. Cathy Guieswite—searchquotes.com
30. Ralph Waldo Emerson—quotationspage.com
31. Agnes Repplier—rightwords.eu

32. Hilary Cooper—goodreads.com
33. Will Kommen—hillmanwonders.com
34. Robert Anthony—brainyquotes.com
35. Albert Einstein—brainyquotes.com
36. Elisabeth Kubbler-Ross and David Kessler in "On Grief and Grieving"
37. George Carlin—en.wikipedia.org
38. Gloria Steinem—brainyquote.com
39. Steven Wright—quotationspage.com
40. David Brent—imdb.com
41. Anon—the Guardian.com article "Don't be so snobby about Wales"
42. H. Jackson Brown Jr—goodreads.com
43. Milton Friedman—goodreads.com
44. Gwyn Thomas—successories.com
45. Anon—searchquotes.com
46. Ambrose Bierce—goodreads.com
47. 48 & 49—Paul Besley—I had the privilege of being trained by Paul when I became a bereavement counsellor with Cruse
50. Natalie Hensby—granted her permission for me to use this
51. Jerome Lawrence—thinkexist.com
52. Marie Curie—goodreads.com
53. L P Hartley—goodreads.com
54. Barbara Ehrenreich—goodreads.com
55. Sheila Graham—the quotationspage.com
56. Jean Giraudoux—bonzasheila.com
57. Anon—cats.info.com
58. Mary Bly—goodreads.com
59. J M Barrie—brainyquote.com
60. Anita Wise—thinkexist.com
61. W. Somerset Maugham—quotationspage.com
62. Anon—idioms.thefreedictionary.com
63. M. Scott Peck—brainyquote.com
64. Alfred Lord Tennyson—bartleby.com
65. Helen Hayes—quotationspage.com
66. Horace Rumpole—qotd.org
67. Anon—wikihow.com
68. Earl Wilson—quotationsbook.com

69. Paulo Coelho—goodreads.com
70. Ashley Montagu—brainyquote.com
71. Billie Burke—brainyquote.com
72. Seneca—quotationspage.com
73. Anon—quotationspage.com
74. Lewis Carroll—brainyquote.com
75. Michael Pritchard—quotationpage.com
76. Kermit the Frog—youtube.com
77. Anon—Jamie.workingagenda.com
78. Lewis Carroll—goodreads.com
79. Kermit the Frog—youtube.com
80. C C Scott—tinybuddha.com
81. 1 Samuel 16.7—biblehub.com
82. Joseph Merrick—en.wikiquote.org
83. Florence Nightingale—saidwhat.co.uk
84. Anon—notmilk.com
85. Mae West—brainyquote.com
86. Emma Thompson—brainyquote.com
87. Paul J Mayer—searchquotes.com
88. Tom Stoppard—goodreads.com
89. Jim Fiebig—thinkexist.com
90. Pele—washingtongreen.co.uk
91. Bill Shankly—dailymail.co.uk
92. Taylor Swift—brainyquote.com
93. Al Pacino—goodreads.com
94. Julian Casablancas—goodquotes.com
95. Pierre Ambroise Francois de La Clos—urbandictionary.com
96. Alfred Hitchcock—goodreads.com
97. Anon—answers.yahoo.com
98. Congreve—phrases.org.uk
99. Stephen King—thinkexist.com
100 Emo Philips—quotationspage.com
101 Bill Cosby—goodreads.com
102 Erma Bombeck—brainyquote.com
103 Phyllis Diller—goodreads.com
104 Erma Bombeck—brainyquote.com
105 Rose Macaulay—quotationspage.com

ACKNOWLEDGEMENTS—December 2013

As ever, my thanks go to Nicky Matravers for her patience and accuracy in proof reading most of this book. I say most as I have a nasty tendency to add more "bits" when I think of them. Any errors will be on my part only!

To Kathleen Scott, Mother, Grandmother, Great Grandmother and a very great friend to two legged and four legged creatures!

To Les and the stud muffin at the London Inn, Othery.

To Café Fleur in Looe for the lovely cream teas.

To the ladies of the Feel Good Factory at the Blackbrook Sports Pavilion for listening and sharing.

To Sarah Soutar—a courageous woman.

To Beverley and her team at the Kings Arms in Taunton who have consistently produced such great lunches for me and my friends.

To PCN Computers who have ridden to my rescue, on three occasions, in order to get this book printed.

To Joy Lake who has sorted out my Inner Child when she comes down with technophobia.

To Jamie Budd, Under Manager of the Coal Orchard—thanks for always being so cheerful and helpful.

To Pauline Drury a good friend who has the solution for everything.

To Jenny Thompson a fairly new friend who is erudite and amusing, we share the same view of housework!

To Becky, Sophie and Ann at my newly discovered "little gem"—The Fountain, Bridgwater.

To the people who bought my previous book and lent to others. Please don't do it again! Writers have to eat.

I would happily have published this book under my own name but have to take into account a family member who values their privacy.

This book is dedicated Tilly Trotter my best feline friend who died on 8 July 2013 and to my best friend Lorraine Summerfield who has cared for me much like her late Mother, Ness. Thank you seems inadequate for all your time, loyalty and chocolate cake!

THE PLAYERS

Quiet Granny—born in the 1880s. She was loved deeply by her Granddaughter Rosie and much admired by her son-in-law, Rosie's Father. Drowned in the river in the 1950s. She had a Scottish funeral, only the men of the family attended the funeral service and the burial. The idea was that the women of the family stayed at home to pray for the soul of the departed. Attending a funeral service helps with the release of grief.

The Fierce Father—born in the 1920's and suffered an abusive childhood. He survived with very little maternal love and found emotions very difficult to deal with. He played football for Charlton Athletic and Bristol Rovers. He had a great love of sport, playing cricket and then golf in later years. He had a very quick brain. He thought "the handicapped child" was very brave when she endured surgery. He was a very honest man even when that made him unpopular.

The Fearful Mother—Born during the First World War and widowed in the Second World War. She once sang in front of 5,000 troupes at Norton Manor Camp. She was a member of a tap dancing group and an industrious and talented needle woman. A very fearful child even when an adult. She could not be too far away from her brothers and sisters. In the 1940's she married a younger go-ahead man. Has a much wanted child who was "damaged in transit"—she called her "my handicapped child". Had several breakdowns and becomes addicted to taking pills of any sort.

The handicapped Child—born in the 1950s. She spent a great deal of her early life in transit when her Mother could not cope or more plastic surgery beckoned. She had ten operations, nine of them on her face. There were many separations from her family. Like her Mother she was fearful and had (has) low self-esteem. She married in the early '70s and had a beautiful daughter in the early '80s.

The Game—Life.

FOREWORD

"Hide not your talents. They for use were made. What's a sundial in the shade? Benjamin Franklin (1).

People who say it can't be done should not interrupt those who are doing it. George Bernard Shaw (2).

I began a journey in the summer of 1997. It was to be one of discovery. There were many points of reference that I needed to visit and re-visit. I set out to discover whether my immutable facts were, in fact, changeable vistas. I had many questions and some of the answers were within me. I needed space and seclusion to sort out the mess I was in. I needed to grow up emotionally. I could never be the same again and that was a blessing, particularly for those who had dealings with me.

I had much loss in my early life and practice does not make perfect when you lose precious people. I lost people through moving, divorce, my own belligerence and the separate suicides of my Mother and Grandmother.

Depression seemed to be handed down in my family and I had spent time in a mental hospital as a voluntary patient in the '70s. So here we have three generations of women who were time warped. Not physically, but emotionally. We functioned in the here and now but dwelt by the rules of yesteryear whose authors are long dead. Each laughed, cried, loved and mourned. All have been kind and cruel, true and false, brave and cowardly. Each life had light and shade, noise and silence.

Two generations have gone and I am left centre stage to write the review. I accept that my critique may not be theirs. The best that could be said for my Grandmother and Mother is that they did what they could with the tools they had. In each of us there is a play without dress rehearsals, encores, re-writes, or a new version once the play is finished. Some of us do not get beyond the first couple of acts physically, and some get no further emotionally.

I was an out of control emotional four year old when I started therapy in my mid 40's. It is, without doubt, the best thing I have ever undertaken. Shortly before my Father died in 1996 he asked "How much longer are you going to remain unhappy?" I never thought that happiness was an option for me. He and I had a tempestuous relationship, but when he became terminally ill we began to appreciate each other and took off the verbal boxing gloves. After his death I decided that I did deserve some happiness.

"Strange Creatures" was intended originally to be about laughter and the male species. I then discovered that my original book "The Diary of a Bunny Boiler" was out of print so I have amalgamated some of it into "Strange Creatures". The combination may not be a marriage made in heaven but both made me who I am today. I'll let the reader decide if it fits or not.

Because I write on topical subjects, I wish to state that I have no intention to cause hurt or offence to any persons because of gender, nationality, colour, creed, disability or sexual orientation. God does have a great sense of humour otherwise why would he give someone with a bilateral cleft lip and palate a Mother who was narcissistic? People who have a lisp or cleft palate will more than understand!

It may seem strange to have a piece about "The End" at the front of the book but, in many ways, the events that happened at "The End" heralded a new beginning for me.

I have sepia photographs of my ancestors, long gone. They form a three dimensional chorus. "She's got ideas above her station. "No one in our family ever wrote a book". Well, maybe it's time someone did! Triumph can come from tragedy and happiness can have its seeds of germination in a dark place. I hope you enjoy this book.

> If you think you are too small to have an impact, try sleeping with a mosquito—The Dalai Lama (3)

THE DIARY OF A BUNNY BOILER

Definition of a Bunny Boiler:—Glenn Close in Fatal Attraction—unstable, a loose cannon, unpredictable, given to boiling bunnies/ruining relationships, especially their own. They are pricklier than any cacti found on the Sierra Nevada desert.

CHARACTERISTICS. Check this list carefully ladies!

Loud, aggressive and overwhelming
Emotionally volatile
Many "friends" but short relationships
Possessive, even with the people they have kicked to the kerb
Quick to anger
Generous, but unwisely and mainly where there is a perceived benefit to the BB
Is a user
Allows self to be used
Adapts easily (but only superficially) to others' wants
Not able to wait for life to happen
Chases the object of desire—stalking in extreme cases
Easily hurt and often misunderstood
Demanding
Unable to see the whole picture—refuses to sit back and reflect
Makes excuses for the behaviour of others when it suits them—their own behaviour is, of course, blameless
Manipulating—will use whatever it takes to gain the advantage
Interferes and entangles themselves in others' "problems"
Hates being alone

Has to be in a relationship—no matter how bad
Goes on trying to revive defunct relationships
Love turns to hate within a very short time
Puts the blame on others continually
Dramatic, vengeful and brooding
Cries easily.

Questions for potential BBs

Do you set it up for your partner to abuse you either physically or mentally/emotionally?

Do you stay in a dysfunctional relationship because you love him, when he is not drinking/hitting you or maybe even when he does? Is this what you think you deserve?

What is your definition of the "good times" you share? If they are all in the past then think again girlie!

Do your friends try to warn you and do you get annoyed when they offer what you know is sound advice?

Are you always there for others—why? Does your involvement and solving of their problems leave you no time for your own and have you engineered that?

Is caution just the warning given to the apprehended villain rather than a tool you can use to help you assess the relationship?

The **good** news—Bunny Boilers are not born they are made.

The **better** news—Bunny Boilers can change!

Neither should we think that Bunny Boilers are always female—this is not the case. However I think females view the male version in a different light.

An aggressive man is:-
Up for it
One of the lads (regarding his treatment of the opposite sex)
He is admired for standing no nonsense from anyone
He is macho
He is mean, moody and magnificent.

Women regard him as the cheeky chappie. They seem resigned to his bad behaviour. How many times have I heard women say "I always go for the bad boys" as though this is set in stone and they have no control of it. We say that "boys will be boys" as if it is a given. We all love Peter Pan, the little boy who never grew up and sometimes we encourage the boy-like behaviour. Peter Pan didn't have a shadow but remember neither did Count Dracula!

THE DAY BEFORE THE END—the late '70s
—but written much later.

> *"Being defeated is often a temporary condition. Giving up is what makes it permanent"—Marilyn vos Savant (4)*

It's amazing how many things I have put in the way of this writing—not just today but over many years. I don't want to think of that time and yet, subconsciously or not, it is frequently on my mind.

That day started with a telephone call from a retired lady Minister at Church. My Mother had been to a coffee morning and, once again, told people she had stomach cancer. I wearily said that I would come and collect her as soon as I could. I was told to stay where I was—she and her friend would give my Mother some lunch and then take her to the Doctors. I breathed a sigh of relief. My Mother had a history of depression, pill-taking and suicide attempts. Here was someone prepared to lighten my load. I will always be grateful for that.

In 1962, when I was twelve, I first became aware of my Mother's pill taking. My Father had gone to visit a nearby neighbour and I was sat in the lounge with my Mother. Her speech suddenly became very slurred and her eyes were not focusing properly. I had my pyjamas on and no slippers. I was just so scared that I flew out of the house and ran to get my Father. He came straightaway and by this time my Mother was in bed and unconscious. He shook her and asked how many pills she had taken and that he would fetch the Police. She was comatose and it was then my Father checked the pill bottle. Not finding any pills missing, he turned his attention to me. My feet were wet and bleeding from the chippings on our drive. He fetched a towel and dried them and then kissed me on the cheek. I almost recoiled, my Father didn't do emotion and my Mother didn't do anything else.

My Father seemed to think that I needed to be near my Mother and tucked me in beside her whilst he slept in my room. Was he abdicating his responsibility as her spouse or did he think it would reassure me? I don't know what his motives were but I knew he was angry. My concern was that if I fell asleep, I might wake up with a corpse next to me.

After my Father left home she sat, like Miss Havisham in Great Expectations, amidst the detritus of her life. I was just someone who dwelt on the periphery of that decay. I would tell her I was going out, who I was seeing and what time I would be back. Wrapped in her own self misery she barely acknowledged my existence.

I have worked, in the past, for government departments, in essence a civil servant. I remember smiling as I read old handwritten letters on the files saying "I remain Sir, your obedient servant". I was certainly my Mother's obedient servant from a very early age and, such was my low self-esteem, I was grateful for any crumb of affection this beautiful creature offered me. I became showered in crumbs but was given nothing of substance. She craved and loved attention and was not particular how she got it. I know the Bible tells us to honour our Mother and Father but I didn't really have a Mother I had a large child.

I get another telephone call to say that the Doctor had suggested Mother should go again into Tone Vale Hospital (the former Cotford Asylum). She had refused all help and was on her way to see me. Literally two minutes later she was stood in my dining room. We were both desperate people. My Mother wanted to stop the pain which would not subside despite the pills she took and I was just so tired of being the rescuer. I challenged her about her refusal to get help and she did what she did best, she starred into the distance and became mute. I asked her again why she didn't want help and, in the ensuing silence, I could feel my anger rising. Whoever said that silence is golden was clearly not experiencing the frustration and sorrow I was. I knew that I wanted to shout at her and physically shake her but I also knew that to do so would have no effect.

I grabbed a letter that needed posting and used that as an excuse to leave her. I said goodbye and got no reply. It would be the last time I saw my Mother alive or should that be existing?

I posted the letter and then went into the George Hotel (a place I had never been before) and sat with a drink, feeling helpless and hopeless. I rang home and my husband confirmed that my Mother was still there and he would take her home and then pick me up. He was so much more than just a good son-in-law to my Mother. He would have done anything he could to help her. She came to live with us for three months the preceding year following another overdose attempt.

On getting home I could not settle and, in the early hours of the next day, I telephoned the Samaritans. I talked and was listened to for almost an hour. I felt a kind of calmness and knew that I would be able to get some sleep.

> *"Our greatest weakness lies in giving up. The certain way to succeed is always to try just one more time"—Thomas Alva Edison (5)*

My Mother and I were both so very tired of trying.

THE END—the late '70s—but written much later.

"And a funeral, I found out is like a wedding in reverse, with less time to plan—J Lincoln Fenn (6)

I awoke to the ringing of the telephone and almost fell down the stairs in my haste to answer it. It was my husband checking to see that I was ok after such a late night. I don't know what I was expecting, but when the telephone rang again, I knew with a surreal certainty that my Mother was dead. I was told only that she had been taken to East Reach Hospital. I knew there was no hurry and it was with a steady adult hand that I dialled their number. They confirmed that my Mother was dead on arrival. I asked what I should do next and was told that the Coroner's Officer would contact me. The Coroner's Officer called and said that a formal identification was needed. He wanted me to have someone with me in case I became distressed as he could not drive and comfort me at the same time. I telephoned my husband and he agreed to leave work early to accompany me. He can remember no detail of the viewing and I can, at times, think of nothing else.

My Mother never went out without lipstick on; she said she felt naked without it. She told me that people who had died just looked as though they were asleep. The sight that greeted me at the mortuary was very far removed from the good looking woman I was used to seeing. My Mother died in a sitting position and her face was badly mottled and discoloured. She looked as though she had been battered. No one had explained lividity, so I was horrified by her appearance. Basically, the blood settles to the lowest place on death. As most people die lying down no one sees this.

If anyone had offered me a million pounds to approach her they would have kept their money. I slept with the light on for quite a while. What I saw haunted me. Two people, in separate attempts to offer comfort, told me that I would see her again probably before the funeral. I rang our Minister to ask about this and he said that some people did say they saw their loved one but he was not sure whether this was because they self-projected this experience. The twelfth of never would have suited me and I have never seen that awful image since. My Mother copied out a poem which spoke of her watching over me from heaven—I would have preferred that she did that on terra firma. The Coroner's Officer had the unpleasant job of asking me if I wanted the nightdress she was wearing. I recoiled in horror but I had to make a formal statement confirming that I didn't want it. Apparently, quite a few people ask for the clothes that are on the body. Maybe they feel that they then have some tangible proof of their loved one's existence or a last connection. Who knows?

Coroner's Officers only do that job for a certain number of years. It must be such a sad job to do particularly when it involves the death of young children. I needed to know that my Mother didn't have cancer and that her intentions were to depart this life. I voiced this to the Officer concerned who confirmed there was no cancer in any of her organs and that there were over 100 undissolved tablets still in her stomach after death. How a Coroner can bring in an open verdict beggars belief. He certainly did me no favours by stating "there was insufficient evidence as to her intention".

Suicide says to those left behind "I can't deal with this, you have it". I have been on both sides of the fence and here I will no doubt lose some readers; suicide is an extremely selfish act. Someone has to find you, to lift the noose from you, to scrape you up, read the suicide note, attend the mortuary and arrange the funeral. A well-known comedienne when asked to comment on her husband's suicide said "What a selfish bastard" and she was right.

That evening my husband handed me a copy of a Will my Mother had made. I was more than surprised. She had always believed that if you made a Will you would die shortly afterwards. She had asked me, about six weeks prior to this, "on behalf of a lady at Church", for the name of a good Solicitor to consult about making a Will. I had worked as a legal Secretary in Hammet Street. I found out, later that year, that she had asked her brother's advice and he told her to leave the most to those who had done the most. Even if she had left me a fortune, (I inherited just under £3,000) I earned every penny. She had asked me, some months before; if I remembered where the family grave was—as if I could forget where my beloved Grandmother was buried. She also said that people should be cremated as it freed up land for housing. (She could be quite grown up at times). So I knew where her ashes would be buried. On another occasion, she told me her favourite hymns. In some ways, she made the unbearable bearable. At least I knew that I had done her bidding, yet again.

Again, a shocking statement; there was some relief when my Mother died—this recurrent behaviour would not happen again. My Mother was constantly offered help but refused it. She ran out of people who would sympathise. Sympathy only helps you to remain a victim. You cannot help anyone you feel sorry for. It wasn't the fault of the medical profession, her friends or her family. I felt that my Grandmother and Mother died defeated and I was determined to break that awful legacy.

> "The willingness to accept responsibility for one's own life is the source from which self respect springs"—Joan Didion (7)

THE "WHAT IFS"—May 1997

These are insidious creatures—they can come in the middle of the night and sometimes by day. They attack the very core of your being. They strip you bare and leave you gasping for breath. They inveigle you into listening to their whispers and before you know it, they are shouting raucously. They paralyse your body and gallop away with your time, energy and potential. The "what ifs" start small and grow to alarming proportions.

You have a niggling ache in your shin, perhaps you have just overdone it today but no, the "what ifs" tell you that your leg is sore, really sore. "They" egg you on to examine your shin with your hand. Is there a lump there? You run your fingers over your skin again. You press harder this time; surely, there is a lump there. You put on the bedroom light and compare one shin with the other—there is a slight difference. That ache becomes an acute pain. There's no way you can go back to sleep. You think of your neighbour, Mrs Jones. She had been so active until the lump appeared. She didn't think it was worth a visit to the Doctor. So she left it alone and the rest is history. An outpatients' appointment turned into an admission and they did talk of letting her home after the amputation but then it spread and everyone said it had been a lovely funeral.

The lump on your right shin is now enormous and you are wondering whether to request donations only and Ave Maria. You have not physically moved from your bed and yet you are dead and buried. The "what ifs" take your today and limit your tomorrows. They feed and breed on the rich compost you give them. You can starve them if you choose but you feed them on all the imponderables and they kill you anyway. I lost my Grandmother and then my Mother because the "what ifs" got them.

> *"I've lived through some terrible things in my life, some of which actually happened"*—Mark Twain (8)

BRACKEN—my cat 1 June 1997

Bracken knows the warmest spot on the landing. She knows when she is full. She knows which brand of cat food she likes best and tells me by leaving the others congealing on her plate.

She grooms her coat until it shines and is then sick because she has swallowed fur balls. Bracken has many moods and not all of them are attractive. On occasion, she will let me stroke her. Once when she was in the mood for stroking and I was not, I removed her from my lap and she bit me. It was a gentle but reproachful bite.

Bracken knows her territory. Bracken knows all the other cats in the neighbourhood. She never picks a fight with those cats she knows are bigger and stronger. Bracken is coldly deferential to these 'superior cats'.

Cats know when changes are coming and the last month before I left the matrimonial home she was glued to my side. She showed me a great deal of love whilst still biting other people!

I think my cat is wonderful. She has the recipe for a successful, long and happy life.

BUT my cat, for some unknown reason, will suddenly decide to cross the road. She does not realise that she is not car resistant. Why she does it even she does not know. AND I know that she will repeat this risky action time and time again.

In my life I have been unroadworthy and have made that mad, frantic dash. I'm the one who is meant to be superior to the cat so WHY do we keep crossing 'those roads'? Perhaps Bracken thinks "I'll give her a scare—she has not fed me today". So she runs and a car narrowly misses her and I gather her in my arms and stroke her. Is this why she runs?—I don't know I'm not a cat.

LEAVING HOME—June 1997

> *"Leaving home in a sense involves a kind of second birth in which we give birth to ourselves"—Robert Neelley Bellah (9)*

The day I left the Old Matrimonial Home was very traumatic and I was the one who wanted to go, or should that be needed to go? I wanted an end to the way we dealt with each other. I decided that the unknown had to be better than the silence between us. I left because the sound of silence had become deafening.

My daughter knew I was looking for a flat and I asked if she would come with me. She was extremely tactful but said that she was in the middle of decorating her bedroom. I do not know, but can imagine, how difficult that was for her. What an impossible choice for her to have to make. I figured that as she was only home at the weekends and in the school holidays then I would probably see quite a bit of her. When she was in Taunton and not with me it was so, so painful and yet it had come about from my choice. When you leave and a child remains behind, then you become an abusive parent.

I never, ever got used to not having her around. Her life undoubtedly changed because of my leaving. I asked a learned friend, at that time, what children could handle and she said "anything but conflict". There was so much conflict between her Ma and Pa that it had squeezed out any love and understanding remaining.

I decided that I needed a drink, to fortify myself. I found a bottle of Jameson's whisky which I had given to my husband as a Christmas present. It was unopened—well it was until that moment. I poured a very generous measure and toasted the debris of our marriage. I took a gulp and it tasted foul. In the fridge was my daughter's bottle of Coke which I used to dilute and disguise the taste. I drank another and another and just got sadder but more resolute. It seemed that I couldn't get drunk but I did bump into quite a bit of furniture. I remember thinking "that's going to hurt tomorrow".

I left the house with my shopping trolley and just a few possessions. It must have been a comical sight for the neighbours as I walked unevenly away from my former life. Leg plaits are not my speciality. My friend Wendy was at her window and asked if I wanted a lift anywhere. She took me to the New Single Me Flat and saw me inside. She said "You're going to be alright" and we both knew that it was a statement not a question.

The settee at the flat was only a two-seater and extremely uncomfortable. I slept on the floor that night—I lagged myself with the Daily Mail. I should have bought The Times as I was over 18 stones and took quite a bit of lagging!

"In the depths of winter I finally learned there was in me an invincible summer"—Albert Camus (10)

MOTORMOUTH June 1997

"I'm so loud, as if I know what I'm on about, but deep inside, I'm so insecure. Just a little girl"—Katie Price (11)

Strength does not have to be belligerent and loud"—Russell Brand (12)

I recall, with sorrow, being motormouth most of my life. I was an aggressive, out of control human Rottweiler. I tended to shout rather than speak and to overrule rather than listen to the other party. When I left the marital home I left behind all the trapping of a 'comfortable' life. I visited Sainsbury's the next day and bought picnic plates and plastic cutlery. Although the New Single Me Flat had a cooker and some furniture, I had no kitchen equipment or utensils.

I knew that matters needed to be discussed and so I invited my husband for tea. I asked him to bring a saucepan to boil the new potatoes in. I bought some sliced ham and salad ingredients. For once, my culinary skills were not to the fore. He was an hour late, he had fallen asleep he said. I was fuming but the Rotti had a new 'psychological choke chain' around her throat. I had to force myself to concentrate on the bigger issue. Slipping into motormouth mode would mean that all would be lost.

He turned up with the saucepan and some of my clothing. He said he had just picked things at random. Believe me, there was nothing random about bringing size 12 clothes when you are easily an 18. The shoes, which all had stiletto heels, had not been worn by me for at least five years. I could feel my anger rising. He asked where he should put the clothes and I was very tempted to tell him. Instead I smiled and suggested he left them on the bed. He sat, uncomfortably, in the dingy lounge. I served the meal and I could see he was unsure of the rational creature in front of him.

During tea and obviously wanting to escape, he asked if I thought he was being fair with the items he had brought. I put a motherly hand on his and confirmed that he had. I could see him thinking "oh bugger, how can I tell her she's being unreasonable and leave when she is not responding to the usual triggers". We discussed what we had to and I wished him a polite goodnight. As a goodwill gesture he left the saucepan—it had belonged to my Mother previously. When I told my counsellor she was delighted and said that I was playing the game. I thought "what game, this is not a time for games?" But indeed it was—I had been a prime player for most of my life. Food for thought eh?

Christmas 2007—Had my then husband been a male bunny boiler he could have torched the lot. Instead, the charity shops did well and I eventually got my 'real' clothes. And, although I was volatile I didn't cut any of his clothes up but boy did I leave him loads of shirts for ironing.

CRAP—my Father's favourite word. 1 July 1997

A wise woman told me a very simple truth and it was the start of me regaining control of my life. I had an appointment to see her to learn some relaxation techniques, but what she said impressed me far more than the techniques. She directed me towards her lounge and when I was seated she stood in the doorway and said "I understand that you've had some crap in your life". In fact she was more explicit in her language but crap will do nicely for the written word! She then said "Did you know that there are two kinds?" I shook my head and she continued "the first is the stuff you can wallow in". (I could certainly recognise that) "The second is one that you can use as manure and grow from it. Now what are you going to do"? It was by far the most challenging and yet exciting piece of advice I had ever been given.

I decided my growth was way overdue and I devised some rules regarding crap.

Crap can be anything that you allow to stop you from reaching your realistic potential.

Crap will mean different things to different people.

Crap can be inherited, if someone tells you crap or says you are crap when you are a 'child' and they are 'the adults' it can stick.

When we buy tomatoes at the supermarket we discard the crap and buy the good tomatoes. So why do we allow emotional, spiritual and physical crap in our lives? Is it because it is familiar, true and valuable or are we frightened that if the crap goes then so do we?

Everyone has some crap in their lives. It is not the amount or the duration that counts but what we do with it.

Crap is easily spread and there is every likelihood that some innocent people will suffer from the crap in your life. It will probably never be the person who actually bequeathed the crap to you.

Crap can be self-inflicted and self-perpetuated. Some people look in the mirror or at others and then declare "I am crap". Crap can overwhelm you if you hang on to it for very long.

As in the Desiderata, there will always be people who have more or less crap than you—remember they too have their story.

You can only deal with your own crap—it cannot be dealt with by proxy. If you deal successfully with your crap you can move on to some gracious living and through that, limit or reject present or future offerings from whatever source.

Crap is universal. It lives and thrives in shops, public houses, offices and factories. The family social gathering is a prime source of rich concentrated crap.

I was once chatting to a relative many times removed. He was a man who had lived a full and challenging life. Through ill-health he was forced to leave a much-loved, very physically active career and take on a sedentary job. In all a worldly, intelligent man. As we supped tea he told me that a well known public school would not have him as a pupil because his Father delivered bread. He had sat a scholarship and passed the examination but not the interview. Was it a kindness for his parents to tell him that, or should they have said "Well, ok you didn't make it but you are still a worthy person".

Elasticated crap can span generations and become your birthright but only if you truly believe it.

If your husband and male maths teacher both had warts and did not treat you well—this does not qualify all men with warts as crap.

If your mother-in-law and ex-wife were fat and gave you crap, it will not necessarily mean that thin women won't give you crap.

If one brother gets in trouble with the police and another brother is consistently late for school you will hear "All the Smith brothers are tarred with the same brush" which we know is, you've guessed it, crap.

BIBLE—August 1997

> *"If you want to know what God thinks about money, just look at the people He gives it to"—Dorothy Parker (13)*

The late Diana, Princess of Wales had a cushion which was embroidered with a message which said If money won't buy you love, you've been shopping in the wrong place—did she buy it in Harrods?

So here I am, sitting expectantly and twitching periodically. I and the settee have both seen better days. I can't tell you what colour it is, too many people for too many years have sat upon it. It looks as weary as I feel. I want to make a 'phone call but don't want to appear too desperate.

Greenslade Hunt has a book auction today and one of my books is in the sale. When I left the Old Matrimonial Home I took with me the family silver—sounds so grand doesn't it? They were actually silver plated pieces, just odd bits, bought by my Father at auctions. Nothing was worth very much but they represented my parents and I had, previously, guarded them well. I was now doing my matrimonial probation in a flat in Trull Road. Trull Road and Park Street seem to be popular places for those who need time out to understand why and how they went wrong.

It seemed incongruous to have silver but no money to pay the rent. The items needed frequent cleaning. They had no practical use and would need to be insured. Break-ins are common in flat-land so, in many ways, they were a liability. The first lesson I learned on leaving the Old Matrimonial Home was that the most important things in life are not things.

When I took the silver to auction I transported it in my shopping trolley. As I wheeled the trolley through the door the receptionist said "What have you got in there, your life"? She didn't realise how accurate she was. The silver auction took place the day the Flower Show was rained off. Vivary Park resembled a boating lake. I had foolishly, not set any reserves to protect my interests and didn't get much money. This was a salutary experience and I was learning fast.

Rent day seemed to come around far too quickly. It seemed that there was always too much month left at the end of the money.

I took to checking the Gazette to see what auctions there were coming up and I spotted a book sale.

There were various books highlighted in the advertisement as being of particular interest. One of the choicest offerings was a Bible published in 1613. I also had a Bible of that date and decided to take it down to have it valued. It was one of two Bibles I had bought as a job lot with some leather-bound books by Charles Dickens. These were the prizes I wanted; the Bibles were just at the bottom of the job lot.

The 1613 Bible had been beautifully kept and looked not to have been opened very often which was a great shame. All that wisdom and the rich language had obviously not appealed to its previous owners. I suspected that it had been kept in a bookcase for most of its life. The book expert was impressed and asked if I was interested in selling it. He said he would put a reserve of a £100 on it. Hence me sitting on the uncomfortable settee, watching the clock to gauge a suitable time to ring whereby I would not be judged too needy by the Auctioneers.

Rent day was approaching fast and I had very little money. I picked up the 'phone and noticed my hand shaking. I could feel the sweat running down my back. It was nervous tension as it was neither warm in or out of the flat. I had to mask my impatience as I spoke to the receptionist. She remembered me and took a note of the lot number. She came back and said "Well, we didn't get a £100 for it". My heart sank, but then she said "We got £500 for it". She seemed genuinely happy for me and I was relieved I would live to fight another day.

I bought these books at a general sale at the Market Hall held by Greenslades in 1966. The job lot was 2s 6d, or to translate for younger readers, 12p!

> *And my God will supply every need of yours . . . .*
> *Philippians 4.19 Holy Bible (14)*

"We have grasped the mystery of the atom and rejected the Sermon on the Mount". Omar Bradley (15)

ALLERGIES—Summer 1997

"Those who cannot remember the past are condemned to repeat it"—George Santayana (16)

Another week should do it. Taking antihistamines I mean. On a bad day I take four Piriton tablets together with a nasal spray, eye drops and three inhalers for hay fever and asthma. Enough of medical matters.

The allergy that was a million times worse than this, was my allergy to "THEM with the dangly bits". I decided they were all the same, much as they say women are when we let them down. I made a pact with myself; I would leave THEM alone and give THEM no reason to bother me. On wearing a new perfume to the office, my boss said it was nice and I said that as she was happily married she should never wear it. It was divorcee perfume— Escape by Calvin Klein.

When we part company with a significant other we need time to lick our wounds and carry on with the mundane things in life that just keep us ticking over. For me, it was a time of mourning and discovery. When you have been "we" for so long you wonder if the "I" is capable of functioning. Even if your marriage has not been successful and you were the one to leave, you will still miss that someone. I felt lost with no one to cook and care for.

I had to rediscover myself. I stumbled around like a newborn colt but 'time out' was essential for me. We know that speed kills, yet we travel at an indecent pace from one fractured relationship to another, dragging the debris of long ago with us. We are needy for the approval we think we deserve. We exchange a defunct love affair for another doomed relationship. We are out there running just to be on the run. Standing still forces us to think and take stock. We often don't like the answers that present themselves to us.

People generally do want good things to happen to you, and when my marriage ended friends and acquaintances all wished that I would meet a suitable "someone". Still smarting from the hurts, real and imagined, I haughtily told them that I was not a bloody lemming. I had spent a quarter of a century throwing myself off the cliff of matrimony and I decided to retire, bloodied yet defiant, to the high ground. I decided to become an honorary lesbian. This means that I hang around with women but I don't touch them!

> *"Bigamy is having one husband too many. Monogamy is the same"—Fear of Flying by Erica Jong (17)*

SMOKEY JOE—1 October 1997

We are ships that pass in the night. We weave in and out of each other's lives. Some people will make a lasting impression good, bad or indifferent. Others will float by us seeming to leave nothing behind. I have a faith that says the best is yet to be and I really hope that there is a heaven for cats.

Smokey Joe was grey, big and beautiful. He didn't ask for much—far less than a human would. He lived with my best friend, Ness and it truly was a 'love affair' between them. He was obviously part British Blue, just so patient and calm. In return for food and shelter he gave companionship, warmth, loyalty and love.

Smokey Joe came into my life at a time when I thought I would never allow anything or person to physically or emotionally touch me again. I was hurting so badly and I think he knew that. He took me for what I was and when I went to bed he cuddled into the back of me.

Maybe it was only the heat he was seeking, but I don't think so. Joe knew I was hurting and he gave me comfort, asking nothing in return. If only humans could do that but we don't, we all have an agenda—a list of "what I want".

Smokey Joe has long gone but he lives on in my heart and memory. I wish for him many slow mice, many free-loving female felines and a warm, soft breeze to give him the warmth and comfort he gave to me.

PHOTOS—June 1998.

"You don't take a photograph. You ask, quietly, to borrow it". Author unknown. (18)

"When you photograph people in colour you photograph their clothes. But when you photograph people in black and white you photograph their souls". Ted Grant. (19)

"You don't want a copy of all of them do you?" said the incredulous voice at the end of the 'phone. "I don't suppose so" I said warily, not understanding the significance of her question. "You see, we have over one hundred photos of you" said the voice. "Well, definitely not then" said I. I had never seen a close up photo of myself as a baby. I had destroyed other childhood photos which showed the scarred, imperfect me.

I was in a discovery and recovery process and the photos would help with that. I arranged a day and time to visit Frenchay Hospital and was told to head for Medical Illustration. Fancy name or what? Back in the 1950's there was just one bloke with a camera and flashlight which temporarily blinded you after taking each photo. The camera and flash were heavy and cumbersome and were loathed by me.

The following extract will give you some idea of how I felt about Frenchay Hospital and what happened to me there. This was the first piece of writing I did when I started my recovery. I have not revised or re-written it for the words are appropriate for the emotional four year old as I was at that time. It was to be over two years before I could read this extract and not cry.

"I was taken from my Mother's arms and given to strangers. The strangers had hands but they were not the same. The hands held me down—they took control—they put a mask over my face and they hurt me. Frenchay hospital is a black, horrid place to me and red is the vivid colour of the rage I felt when I was left there. Red was the colour of the black and white photos of me—the worst part of me. Red was the colour of my lip, palate and nose. The pain was red raw. Red was the colour of the taunts, jibes and sneers which echoed through the playground and through life. The rage was red—I cannot bleach that colour out. I was orally raped by a technician's camera before and after each operation. The rage inside shouted "I am here behind the nose and the scars" but I did not cry out when it hurt. I would not have liked the smells, sounds and touches when I first went there and I would have recognized them again when I returned for another operation. I would have learnt that to cry was futile. I would have heard other babies crying and not being comforted. I would not have liked that sound. When I was little I realized that ugly people were not sent away to be mended and so I thought I was worse than ugly. As soon as I was able to speak my Mother insisted that I thanked the nurses for what they had done—betrayal or what?"

No one was cruel to me but I was treated like a medical specimen—I was reduced to the size of my deformity. I was always willing to co-operate with the photographer. I would think "yes, let him take the photos and it will soon be over. I can then escape to the place in my head where I am normal".

I digress, back to visiting Medical Illustration. I decided that I needed to be business-like and slightly distanced when I went to view my life in hospital captivity. I arrive, with my cheque book in hand. The photos were set out on a large table in sets. I select six photos which spanned the years. I thanked the member of staff and passed over my completed cheque. As I was heading towards the door, she said "Lots of people do what you are doing now". I asked what she thought I was doing. A bit of an amateur psychologist, she said "Well, you are in your forties and you are trying to reconcile your life". Too right I was.

She told me that the photos would arrive in two to three weeks. I gave her the address of the Old Matrimonial Home. These photos were too precious to rely on delivery to bed-sit land. Post would often go missing and you never really knew who you were sharing the house with. My ex-husband, very kindly, delivered the envelope but I delayed opening it until I was quite alone. Oddly enough, the first photo of me at about the age of three months asleep left me quite cold. I guess I couldn't actually identify with the sleeping babe. The photo of me aged four showed a wide-eyed child with resignation and oh so much sadness in her eyes. I wanted to envelop her in my arms and hold her until she felt safe.

Several years later . . . .

Some days are better than others—the young man at the bus stop proved that. I waited for my bus and he decided that I was "it" for today. He took the rip out of me about the size of my nose and the scars on my lip. The comments hurt and I wanted the ground to open up and swallow HIM! I can do little about the comments of others. On a good day I can be generous and allow the stares and comments to wash over me. I tell myself that I am a better person than they are. On a bad day, such as today, I want to lash out and then run and cry my eyes out. I don't do any of these things at the bus stop but the tears pour once I am inside my own front door. Does it help some people to feel 'one up' on those who look different?

"The camera can photograph thought"—Dirk Bogarde (20)

"A photo is usually looked at, seldom looked into"—
Ansel Adams (21)

STARTING OVER—1 November 1997

It's a long and painful process even for the one who makes the final decision. For those people who have been part of a redundant relationship for many years it is fraught with danger. Suddenly, you are forced "to start over". Perhaps you've allowed your figure to sag and you have got out of the habit of "making yourself look nice". Then it happens, wham, bam you are back on the market again. Time out is good advice for all.

Being on the market is much more perilous than when you were young. The newer models have indulged themselves in looking younger for longer. Keen, lean and much, much more mean. There are women who will settle for less than you. There will be women who are attracted to the man you have kicked to the kerb. This will bring about some confusing emotions. This is called the "I don't want him but you can't have him" syndrome.

The dating game is a trap for the unwary when you reach your half century and have had a previous long relationship. Your dance card was full up almost twenty five years earlier—it had been thrown to the back of a drawer when you said "I do". There will be men who will offer a shoulder to cry on but make sure that shoulder is covered in a shirt and not inhabiting a double bed. Your ego doesn't need a second bashing from an "understanding" friend.

If you indulge in online dating you will be surprised by the number of men who are cohabiting but looking for "fun". Perhaps they are the honest ones. How many men put themselves up as being single and are in fact, married? You will be amazed at the huge number of potential dates who earn between £45,000 and £75,000 and yet still live in a Council flat! I guess what I am saying is that all that glitters is not gold.

So is it to be one lone ego or two? One ego can wear unflattering but warm nightgowns and bed socks. You can have a hot water bottle that is guaranteed to stay hotter for longer than any man. Wearing big pants doesn't mean you don't love him anymore. No one cares if your underwear is not co-ordinated. Television can be switched on or off and no one is channel hopping with the remote control. Meals contain the favourite ingredients of the lone ego. It is true to say that there are no cuddles and so your gas/electricity bills may increase but weigh this up against potential heartbreak and then alter your Direct Debit to cover the rise in cost. I am a believer in never saying never but it would take an extraordinary man for me to trade in my independence. I have recently made a commitment to living alone—I've fitted my necklaces and bracelets with magnetic clasps. I no longer spend nights sleeping in a necklace which I can't manage to remove.

P.S. When you live alone flatulence is no longer a problem!

THE INTERPRETATION OF INTERNET AND TELEPHONE DATING FOR THE UNWARY WOMAN

Having, in the past, dabbled in the above I thought I should shine some light on the phrases used and their meaning. I could describe myself as "cuddly" when I am actually obese. I would also say that I am "bubbly"—well after I have consumed copious amounts of alcohol this may be true. Enough of me, let's get started!

Medium build—definitely obese.

Stocky—morbidly obese and looking for a potential carer.

Salary over £75,000 per annum—I am a fantasist and a liar.

Loves sport—you will never get to watch any of your soaps while there is any kind of sport on TV.

DIY enthusiast—I am tight and refuse to pay a professional to do a proper job and I have never completed a DIY project.

Healthy outdoor type—you will need to wear your coat indoors in the winter. I won't put the central heating on until hell freezes over!

Loyal—I never date more than three women at once.

Lively—I can manage to stay awake until the news at ten.

Rugged good looks—I can't be arsed to shave.

Athletic—I spend hours looking at myself in a full length mirror.

Extrovert—I have a leopard print posing pouch.

Adventurous—I would like a threesome with another woman.

Age, nationality and size not a problem—I will screw anything that moves.

Looking for a genuine woman—transsexuals need not apply.

A fan of motor sport—but don't expect me to mow the lawn.

Easy going man who enjoys staying in—I have a tag fitted with a curfew from 8 pm until 10 am.

Hardworking—don't expect any help with the housework.

Faithful type—surely there must be someone who fancies me.

Considerate—I always apologise when it is obvious that I've farted and the dog is nowhere around.

Loves countryside pubs—can't take you out in town in case someone tells my wife.

Interested in conservation—I would rather spend your money than mine.

Good looking—well my Mother says I am.

Tactile—I will grab your boobs whenever I feel like it.

Very tactile—I don't mind grabbing them in front of other people.

Looking for fun times—the minute you have a problem I am out of here.

Great sense of humour—I laugh at all my own jokes and like to poke fun at others.

Uncomplicated—I've had 3 wives and I can't count past 10.

No ties—the Child Support Agency have not got my new address.

Loves photography—get your kit off while I take some page 3 shots.

Solvent—I collect my Job Seekers Allowance regularly.

Car boot enthusiast—I refuse to have treatment for my hoarding.

Quiet natured—I am good at sulking.

Music lover—I am great on air guitar.

Enjoys good food—don't pick me if you can't cook.

Loves cosy times—the closer we can get the lower the central heating control gets.

Looking for a realistic, sympathetic woman—I'm not interested in you but can talk for hours about me, myself and I.

PHILIP—September 1998

Philip arrived on time, his pink face scrubbed and shiny. He came bounding up like a new puppy. He didn't have 'desperate' tattooed on his head but he might as well have. He was effusive and slightly sweaty. Obviously not an exponent of the 'less is more' ethos as he had had a run-in with several bottles of aftershave. Once we agreed that we would "go Dutch" for the drinks we settled down for an evening of stilted conversation and long silences.

I think you know straight away if you 'click' with someone and, as far as I was concerned, it was 'clunk' and not 'click'. He was obviously yearning for a relationship but I didn't feel flattered as I think that King Kong would have been in the running if he was available and wore lipstick.

For some reason, Philip thought he would shorten my name to Ro. Every question started with "Well Ro . . .". It was irritating and I found myself looking at my watch whenever he went to fetch a drink or answer the call of nature. It was only a couple of hours but it felt like weeks. The only positive thing that I could say about the evening was that, eventually, it would come to an end. As soon as was politely possible, I made movements to leave and he wanted to walk me home. I didn't want him knowing where I lived so I said there was no need as it was only a minute's walk away.

I said that it had been nice to meet him and he lunged forward and planted a wet, sloppy kiss on my lips. I made a mental note to wipe my mouth once he was out of sight. He obviously felt satisfied with this and started to talk about a second date. I smiled, thinly, and said that I had a hectic social life and couldn't make any plans at present. The penny dropped and he ambled slowly away concentrating on his mobile 'phone. Maybe he was looking for Kong's number—if Kong liked aftershave they could waltz away into a happy future together. On regaling a friend with the details she said I should have told him that my name was Rosie and not Ro. To be honest, I knew I would never eat breakfast with him so it was unimportant.

GETTING OVER IT! Christmas 1999

"It always struck me in years after how bizarre it was, how two people could look at one another with such tenderness and complete love, and how quickly that could dissolve into nothing but bitterness"—Hannah Harrington—(22)

Today I went to buy a Christmas present for my ex-husband. He has offered to cook me a meal and he doesn't owe me any favours. I accepted his invitation and will get him a gift he might appreciate. I decide to buy some nice aftershave, you know the sort that you keep promising yourself when you have some spare cash. But that day never seems to come—there is always something more important to spend your money on.

I find myself at the counter of a store in town which sells delicious perfumery and aftershave. The lady behind the counter looked stunning. Around my age, her make-up was flawless, her hair beautifully coiffured. She was slim with a beaming smile.

She asked me if I would like my purchase gift wrapped and it was while she was doing that I said "I never thought I would be buying a Christmas present for my ex-husband". Well, the change was immediate and startling. She hissed, through clenched teeth, "If my ex-husband walked into the store now, on fire, I would not p . . . s on him to put the fire out!"

I looked at her square-on and then remembered how bitter I had been for about eighteen months after I left my marriage. I said

"Obviously, this is a recent split?" "No" she spat "it was ten years ago". I went on to say that there were some nice men out there. Again, the clenched teeth and "Well I've never met any!" and something told me she never would. As I walked away she said "Sorry about the language" but that really wasn't the problem was it?

> *"Work like you don't need the money, love as though your heart has never been broken, and dance as though no one is watching you."—Satchel Paige (23)*

> *My Grandmother always told me; beauty fades, but dumb is forever" Judge Judy (24)*

DIARY OF A DESPERATE DIETER—May 2001

> *"Inside me lives a skinny woman crying to get out. But I can usually shut her up with cookies." Unknown (25)*

If my body is a holy temple why do I treat it like the town dump? Is it that each time I over eat I am re-affirming my dislike for myself? That's food for thought—damn, it's the f word again!—Rosie.

Have you noticed that people on diets only talk about food? Dieting requires stamina and I always try to eat a really crusty pork pie while reading the blurb for the new wonder diet. Why should dieting be so difficult? Why does will-power surrender at the thought of a custard doughnut? A moment on the lips, an inch on the hips. I have, in the past, tried to convince my Doctor that I have an under active thyroid gland—I mean it couldn't be ME to blame could it?

I got on the scales today and they screamed "Ouch will one of you get off!" I decide to list the benefits and drawbacks of going on a diet. So here goes:-

BENEFITS

1. My asthma would be better.
2. I would look more attractive.
3. I would feel healthier.
4. I could get into my jeans again.
5. My back would improve and I would not need to visit my Osteopath so often.
6. My confidence would improve—I always feel more positive when I am thinner.

AGAINST

There are no pitfalls—damn!

If I am to diet I will need to develop more control over my habit—food has become my fix (amongst others) and is a much more acceptable method of self destruction/reward than heroin or cocaine.

8.15 am—I arrive at work—I am going to start my diet today—no—I have started my diet today. I will have All-Bran and skimmed milk with artificial sweetener for breakfast and an apple. I greet my colleagues as they arrive but do not meet their gaze as I am too busy taking in details of their lunchboxes.

9.55 am—I am looking at our internal transit envelopes and wonder what they would taste like with a smear of Marmite on them. I have placed photos of a thinner me on my desk.

10.30 am—I have poured the All Bran into a bowl—should I pretend it is a bowl of super deluxe muesli with nuts and loads of brown sugar? I might try but my taste buds are just not prepared to countenance such deception.

1.30 pm—Lunch is a piece of wholemeal toast lightly spread with Bertolli and some reduced calorie baked beans—not many. I'm not saying I could eat a horse but a Shetland pony would be quite acceptable—grilled, of course, not fried!

6.00 pm—I have eaten all my meals and there is just too much day left at the end of the calories! I decide to watch a fitness video I bought many years ago. I straighten up from loading the video and decide I need a rest. Maybe just watching will burn off some calories particularly if I use the control to rewind and fast forward. There is an instructress who has never had a weight problem. I take an instant dislike to her and her outfit. Tomorrow I will start doing the exercises.

> *"I'll think of it tomorrow . . . . after all tomorrow is another day"—Margaret Mitchell (26)*

Some Rosie tips on weighing yourself:-

Don't weigh every day
Always weigh (if possible) naked and first thing in the morning.
Remove all jewellery.
Take out any dentures.
Clear ears of wax.
Remove any belly button fluff.
If you have just had a bath and hair wash—make sure your hair is bone dry. If you can arrange to have it cut as well that would help.
Make sure you have been to the toilet—Number 1 and 2!
If you are feeling desperate shave your legs, underarms and any other bits you fancy.
Cut finger and toe nails.
Blow your nose really hard.
Pluck your eyebrows.

I don't think this diet is going to be very successful but I can recommend a really good and simple diet—don't eat anything you like—Rosie

Why can't they make lettuce taste of pizza/chocolate/cheese etc—Rosie

Knowledge is knowing that a tomato is a fruit

Wisdom is not putting one in a fruit salad—Miles Kington (27)

"Nothing tastes as good as skinny feels"—Kate Moss (28)

GUILT—September 2001

"Food, love, careers and mothers—the four major guilt groups—Cathy Guisewite (29)

I could have cited oven chips as being part of the irretrievable breakdown of my marriage.

Prior to my leaving my husband in June 1997, I stopped doing a lot of things. I let the ironing pile up. I didn't clean the house. Every night when my husband came home he would ask "What's for tea?" It was always oven chips. I am a good cook. I loved dinner parties and I would always keep a note of what people had eaten to make sure they got a different meal when they came again. I enjoyed the challenge of new recipes and ingredients. Week-day meals were always more of a chore when I was working, but I made the effort. I made my own ice-cream, created a lot of soups and home-made pies. I think women of my generation were expected to be able to accomplish that.

Suddenly, oven chips became the extent of my repertoire together with whatever meat there was in the freezer. My heart had gone out of that home (or should I say, house). We lived apart; we had our own bedrooms and a great deal of misery. We were both isolated in our loneliness. We both came from families where respectability was everything. I thought that my disinterest in housework and cooking was because of my depression. Depression came to be a very handy "catch all" for my doing/not doing/coping/not coping. My first flat left a lot to be desired and I was sat in the lounge one evening when I noticed a cobweb. I immediately climbed up on a chair to remove it. It occurred to me that my depression obviously didn't extend as far as my new abode.

My ex-husband and I are now friends—but we were not even that when we were married. He is now an excellent cook.

So, yes I feel guilty about oven chips—I guess it was my protest— my offering for the funeral feast of our marriage.

SORRENTO—September 2001

> *"Do not follow where the path may lead*
> *Go instead where there is no path and leave a trail"*
> *—Ralph Waldo Emerson (30)*
>
> *"The impulse to travel is one of the hopeful symptoms*
> *of life"—Agnes Repplier (31)*

The journey from Naples was tiring and I was very much looking forward to seeing my room at The Grand Hotel Hermitage, just outside of Sorrento. I was disconcerted that I was actually given a room at the Villa Romita, which was up a steep hill from the main hotel. Actually it was a blessing as some guests said that the hotel was noisy at night. My room was cool, inviting and on the second floor. Someone from the hotel sat in the lobby at night so I felt reasonably safe.

Joining me, as residents of the Villa, were two couples who had met on a previous holiday and now travelled together. They were on the floor below me and to the left. At the same time as me, they too threw back the shutters and stood out on their balcony to enjoy the view from what felt like the top of the world. Eventually, three of my fellow travellers disappeared back inside leaving just one gentleman on the balcony. Thinking himself alone, he let out one of the loudest farts I've ever heard. No, I didn't cough or laugh out loud but I did vacate my balcony very quickly—well hot air rises doesn't it?

I was the only person who was on their own at the hotel. I had my own small dining table and was invited each and every night to join others if I wished. I liked people watching from my vantage point but joined the others in the bar after dinner for drinks and pleasant conversation.

I had signed up for a tour of Capri which I had visited before. Someone had noticed another lady on their own at another hotel used by the travel company. No doubt they had the best of intentions in throwing us together on that trip, but I would like to have been consulted first. The lady was slim and quite a stunner but did nothing but moan and bitch about her lot in life. I had booked another trip to Amalfi and Ravello but the thought of another whole day in her company was untenable. I decided a chill-out day doing nothing would suit. I discover that the Villa has a flat roof ideal for sunbathing. Even the small green lizards took their time in passing.

The tour guide told us about Orlando's bar in the nearby village of Sant Agata. Apparently, there had been an injured, homeless cat nursed by the owner. The cat, called Sherpa, ever grateful for being adopted, did an acrobatic act with its saviour and was also known to enjoy the odd cigarette. Goodness knows what the RSPCA would have said but that was back in the early '60s. I sought the bar out one hot afternoon and enjoyed a lager which lasted quite some time. It seemed that the Italians, as well as the French, have no problem with a customer lingering over a drink. The Landlord gave me a photo of Sherpa with his Father and it is propped up close to my laptop as I write this.

> *"Life is not measured by the number of breaths we take but by the places and moments that take our breath away"—Hilary Cooper (32)*

> *"If you look like your passport photo, you're too ill to travel"—Will Kommen (33)*

RISK—21 March 2002

Today is arctic—I can't zip up my jacket because of my burgeoning weight gain resulting from two recent holidays and the fact that I am a glutton.

I make the decision (yet again) that I should catch the bus to work. As usual, I have come up with valid reasons for this. I have extolled the virtue of bus travel as giving employment to people—after all, if we didn't use the buses what would the drivers do to earn money? I stop myself inventing these excuses—bottom line—I don't want to walk to work.

I walk to the bus stop feeling guilty and double-fat. The daffodils are out, glorious, yellow and proud. They have taken the risk of daring to be. They have flowered because it is their time. They stand defiant. The wind chill factor must threaten them. There may still be the risk of snow. There has been, for the past two years, a mindless idiot who has walked the length of them stripping their heads as he/she goes. But the blooms refuse to give in.

Risk is a frightening thing but it is necessary if you are to triumph at anything in life.

> *"Most people would rather be certain they're miserable than risk being happy"*—*Robert Anthony (34)*

> *"A person who never made a mistake never tried anything new"*—*Albert Einstein (35)*

HE WHO WILL NEVER BE FORGOTTEN —7 January 2003

> *"The will to save a life is not the power to stop a death"*—*Elisabeth Kubler-Ross and David Kessler (36).*

I sat in the Old Library two nights ago. You were very much a creature of habit and so I waited and you didn't come.

When we broke up, I purposely took a different route to work, firstly to avoid your anger. The anger you felt was voiced in the messages you left on my 'phone shortly after the break. I was also not sure that I could remain strong if I saw you. So we broke up on the weekend of the Queen's Golden Jubilee in June 2002. I remember going home and sorting out clothing and documents as though I was having a spring clean. I wrote to you but did not express myself in a way that you would have understood.

You were just so dominant and I didn't know how to ask for what I wanted. We always did what you wanted—I did not ask for things, because I had never been shown how. That was not your fault or mine—we can thank our parents for that, but it was inevitable that I would resent this. We parted because you wanted to stay where you were and I wanted more.

I'm listening to "Gone Country" with Mandy Parker and Ted Turner (or rather Chris Hardcastle). I bought you a copy of it for your birthday. I wonder who has that now. I remember early in 1998 hiking my overloaded shopping trolley up the stairs at No. 22. You heard and came out to offer assistance and the Independent Woman said to He Who Will Never Be Forgotten "I can manage, I'm an independent woman". When I actually got into my bedsit and repositioned my dislocated shoulder I decided I had to stop being Mrs Ironbritches. I felt that I was allergic to them with the dangly bits, but I acknowledged that I needed to get beyond that and you were the catalyst.

You used to leave the door of your bed-sit open and when you played your 12 string guitar, the music floated upstairs and reminded me of the sixties. If the music played then I danced and my daughter now carries on that tradition. Anyway, I wrote you a note which ended by saying "As Abba said, thank you for the music". Corny, yeah I know. You wrote back asking me if I would like to go out for a drink. Well, I had lost a great deal of weight and knew just the dress to wear. I wanted to wear a dress that was not part of my old life and I had one in the wardrobe which I had never worn before.

I was excited and nervous. We had a smashing day and I felt so proud to be looking good and part of a couple again. We had loads of banter, told jokes and laughed. I hadn't laughed in a long time and neither had you. However, we had both been hurt in the past (and caused a great deal of hurt in return)—two sensitive souls were bound to have quite a few partings. When these happened I could not cope and would spend hours in tears. People at work and friends were extremely patient with me.

I remember once we were invited to a birthday party at the Victoria pub in East Reach and I made an entry in my diary followed with the letters IWASS. You asked what that meant and I said it stood for "if we are still speaking". As I said, we had many partings but some really fabulous making ups.

One Saturday morning I asked if you would like a bacon sandwich and your eyes lit up! I said I would bring the food down as you had a table and I did not. When I looked in my fridge I found bacon, eggs, sausages and mushrooms. When you saw the plates you said that the Somerset bacon sandwich was definitely preferable to the one served in the North. We enjoyed the impromptu feast and then you said "You've left a mushroom on your plate". My Mother and yours would have been so pleased with the look of reproof on your face. I said "Would you like to eat it or parcel it up and send it to a Third World country?" You smiled because you were also a post Second World War baby and plates had to be empty.

My best friend at that time was called Lin. I remember the evening we met way back in 1966. I was living at the YWCA at the time and as I walked down the staircase on my way out I heard a voice say "That's a lovely dress". Lin had just moved down from London. We forged a firm friendship which lasted many years. She was my bridesmaid and I was her witness and we saw each other through some good and bad times. If you were to be my significant "other" then you needed to meet Lin.

We arranged a time and you decided to play the confident "I can pull any bird" role. You winked at her when she arrived and then went to get some drinks. On your return, I saw you wink at her again. We spent a pleasant hour together and then I headed to the ladies. On my return, Lin said she had to go. You and I had another drink and then headed back to bedsit land. On the way home you said that you didn't like Lin and I asked why. Your reply made me hoot with laughter. After all the winking from the man about town she asked if you had something wrong with your eye. A former partner of mine, apparently when I was out of the room, used to list all the things that he had done for me in recent times and instead of the pat on the head, which was expected, she said "Well, why not, you are her partner after all". Lin was direct and told the truth and sometimes it was the naked truth!

You were prone to some very black moods and I was no stranger to them but maybe I was starting to recognise and manage mine. I remember you went late night shopping and came back depressed because everyone seemed to be having a good time except you. I've done the same thing on occasion but have to admit that if you purposely put yourself in a situation where you know you will feel some pain then it is entirely your own fault. Mankind is not going to change to accommodate your moods and maybe, just maybe, they are having a worse time than you.

One Saturday we had planned to go to the Westgate Inn to hear some music. I was really looking forward to it and then you came up to my bed-sit to say that you were not in a happy mood and would not be going after all. I can remember sitting on the edge of my single bed thinking "oh another lonely evening in". Then I glanced at my left hand and realised there was no wedding or engagement ring there. We had only known each other a few weeks.

I rang Lin and we set off to enjoy a good evening. There was a duo playing and playing well. During their break they came over and introduced themselves as John and Malcolm. Malcolm was the one who set up all the equipment and did the sound checks. It almost seemed that John was the star attraction rather than part of a team. Malcolm did not seem to have much emotional intelligence as he was younger than me and on his fourth marriage. They wanted us to hang around and have a drink with them once they had finished their gig. No doubt this was why Malcolm had had so many wives.

Part way through the second half Lin said she didn't care for the look of mine and I said that hers was nothing to write home about either. Very naughtily we left with a wave of our hands and no backward glance. We had enjoyed our evening and the music. You joined me for a cuppa the next morning to regale me with your woes. You saw my red dress thrown on the back of the settee and asked if I had worn it last night. I confirmed that I had and you said "You look really great in that dress. It's my favourite." I told him that John and Malcolm thought I looked good in it too and after that I can't remember you cancelling an evening out.

One evening at the Westgate Inn you told me that you had made a request for the band to play a song and had dedicated it to me. I was thrilled but the smile froze on my face when they sang "Help me make it through the night". "Oh no" I thought "another bloody person who wants me to rescue them". When I had emotional needs you were "not available" and would leave my presence if I shed any tears. In many ways it was all about you and I could recognise it after parenting my Mother.

We shared passion and it was always in your bedsit as I only had a single bed. I always returned to my own room at some early hour of the morning and it bugged you that I would not stay the whole night with you. One Saturday you had cooked a breakfast and afterwards you stood with your arm on the ornate Victorian mantelpiece looking extremely confident and self assured. Well I couldn't allow that to remain could I? I said that I had given the matter some thought and agreed to stay the whole night in your bedsit. Your face showed the fact that you thought "well it was only a matter of time." I lowered my eyes and asked you to confirm that you were a man of the world. Your arm moved from the mantelpiece. You reluctantly said that you were. I decided to drag it out for a bit—and said that you had been round the block a bit and you were broadminded. By this time the smile had left your lips and I could see that you were checking me over to see if any bits of me were false and liable to be unscrewed if I stayed the whole night. I said that I would need to bring something with me that night; a kind of marital aid. You asked what kind and I thought I had kept it going long enough and said "Well an iron and an ironing board because you need to learn how to iron a shirt. The one you're wearing looks bloody awful". You laughed and said "I know how to iron I just don't like doing it". I said "Darling, I could marry you tomorrow; we just have so much in common."

I remember we were 'apart' on my birthday and you rang and asked if I was going out to celebrate. I said that Lin and I would be going up to the Westgate for a drink. You told me you would drop by and share a "swift pint". Apart from picking up some clean clothes I think I went home from your place about four days later! We shared such passion and immense tenderness, yet we could both be vitriolic and wounding when we sparred. Eventually you said that even if we did fall out you knew it wouldn't last for long 'cos we were meant to be together. It breaks my heart to recall that.

The Old Library is now called the Pitcher and Piano and is painted that bloody awful grey colour that Humbrells used to make for painting model aircraft. You would be pleased to know that the Natraj is still open and serving superb curries. Do you get curry in heaven?

Why oh why did you have to go—it was your decision. You had had pneumonia when you were twelve and were intelligent enough to know that you were ill. You can even be vaccinated against it now. You just didn't want to go on living did you? I had already lost two precious people who brought an end to their own lives—did you have to emulate them? A colleague asked you if you were suicidal and you said that you were fatalistic—I'm not sure there's much of a difference.

All I have now are photos, part of an airline ticket when we went to Ottawa and precious, precious memories. You were my Indian summer—I am just so very glad that I met you and shared some of your time.

I went to the Old Library that night and waited for you. You didn't come and now you never will.

WOMAN ON PHONE—1 April 2004

I had an appointment to see my Counsellor today. I look forward to this. We generally don't plan the session or maybe that's the way I am meant to see it. We know each other well and she puts up with no rubbish from me. I am sure that, on occasions, she would like to strangle me.

Before my appointment I decide to do some shopping. I like to have a wander around Primark. When they opened their new larger store in town, I took the day off which really puzzled He Who Will Never Be Forgotten. I had actually decided to take the day off anyway. I told him that, as I spent so much money on their goods they would probably expect me to cut the ribbon and declare the store open.

When he and I next spoke I explained that they had obviously got someone else to cut the ribbon and, in a fit of pique, I had circumnavigated the store and then left without purchasing anything! I don't think he realised that I was pulling his leg.

So here I am, once again, looking around Primark. There is in front of me, a very harassed woman with a young child and an insistent mobile 'phone. She answers tersely and just says "Yes" several times. As she put the 'phone back in her bag, she says, loudly, to the child and onlookers "How am I ever going to get the shopping done if she keeps ringing me?" Well the answer was clear to me; turn off the mobile 'phone. But, of course, there was some mileage in not turning it off. She was in "victim" mode and two things occurred to me.

1. How could she appear harassed without harassment and
2. If she failed to get the shopping done or forgot something then she would not be the one to blame.

During the counselling session I tell my counsellor of this incident and she praises me for my observation. I bristle with pride and self-importance. It is only on getting home that I realise I've been out wearing a bright pink top with red lipstick on. As I am not Christine Hamilton, who has a penchant for wearing these two colours together, I bolt the door in case Trinny and Suzannah are coming to get me. Conclusion: Woman who wears the wrong lipstick should not point out others' failings!

STEPHEN—28 May 2004

If Stephen had been a woman, I would have described him as a "vision of loveliness". As he walked towards me, his expensive clothes and air of breeding showed. "Why", I asked myself, was such a beautiful man using a dating agency?" I was about to find out.

We had opted to meet for a coffee in a safe, public place during the day. We got our beverages and chose a table that afforded us some degree of privacy. I didn't have to fill any silences because there were none. Stephen, obviously, had a great need to be heard.

It was definitely a one-way conversation which was surprising, given the fact that I can be rent-a-gob. It turned out that Stephen had had a unique experience and obviously felt the need to preach to the unconverted. "Good," I thought, "a spiritual man". Was he C of E or Roman Catholic? Neither. It turned out that Stephen had had an "out of the body" experience.

He was still holding forth and waxing lyrical when he saw my eyes glaze over. He offered me more tea but I think I had heard enough about auras and the like. Let's face it girls when you are sat opposite a hunk it's not an out of the body experience that's on your mind is it?

FRENCHAY TALK—31 January 2005

"I'd love to" said my evil twin when "we" were asked to give a talk. As part of my therapy, I wrote about my experiences and feelings concerning Frenchay Hospital. It has gone from a bleak, black place to one that is not so threatening. I still feel sadness when I visit and think of all the patients that I knew who had undergone painful and frequent surgery. So many people show such courage about "being and looking different". I guess many of them, like me, didn't have a choice—you know the "sink or swim" ethos.

About 12 years ago I was offered an appointment with James Partridge who founded the charity "Changing Faces". He was involved in a car crash as a young adult which left him with severe facial burns and scarring. Straightaway the vitriolic Rosie said "Is there any chance that he will pass his burns on to his grandchildren?" So that was the end of that—boy did I need some counselling together with a kick up the arse!

Having written out my rage about my face I sent it to Outlook which is a psychological support service for anyone affected by a disfigurement or is visibly different. I was contacted by Tina Owen and asked if I would give a talk at a meeting that was taking place at the Bristol Royal Infirmary. This was when Motor mouth (the evil twin) spoke up for the two of us. I drafted out what I was going to say and then sent Tina a copy. I had never spoken publicly before. I caught a very early train to Bristol and killed time in a café having a nice breakfast. I was extremely nervous but the subject matter won and I explained how I felt about Frenchay in the 50s/60s. The round of applause was genuine and not just polite. Tina said there were some very moist eyes when I spoke of my deepest feelings. That evening I was due to take part in a treasure hunt but I was totally exhausted and wrung out. I was so glad that I had done it though. "That's put that one to bed" or so I thought.

Tina contacted me again and asked if I would give a talk at Frenchay to the Cleft Team. This included nurses, plastic surgeons, speech therapists, paediatricians and psychologists. An illustrious bunch which would have fazed the old Rosie. The evil twin won again and couldn't wait to prepare her speech. I went to Frenchay on 31 January 2005. It's a day that I will never forget. I gave my talk and it was well received. Some members of staff could remember the almost communist regime of Ward 30.

I arrived home and there was a message on my answer phone. It was from my best friend's daughter asking me to ring back. I delayed doing so sensing that it was going to be bad news and indeed it was the worst kind. My best friend Ness, who championed me for years, had passed away. Ness was quite the most incredible person I have ever known. Her beginnings were not good; she was fostered from the age of two but never adopted. She had come to a moment in her life when she wanted to know more and luckily she had an excellent Health Visitor who helped her to apply to Dr. Barnardos for details of her parentage. Her Mother had died very young and her Father was left with three very young children to look after. Today he would have got all the help he wanted to stay at home and be their chief care giver, but not in those far off days. The children became Barnardo's children.

All my best friend ever wanted was to have a picture of her Father—he died just four years prior to Ness making enquiries.

She never got that photograph and it still makes me weep. Ness was an out and out giver. She was truly a rare and loving person. She lived next door to us in the'60s and she and my Mother became good friends. She was quite a bit younger than my Mum and quite a bit older than me. She was unique in that she loved my Mum but still allowed me to have my valid but bitter feelings about my past.

Ness encouraged me with my writing and told me to get on with it so that she would be around to see my work published. I hesitated too long and in an instant she was gone. I could not be there to say goodbye to her but I was doing the next best thing. I was reclaiming my past and "telling it the way it was" at Frenchay Hospital. I know she would have been proud of me. Whenever I spoke to Ness we would always finish the call by saying "I love you" and I have taken my lead from her. Each time I speak to my daughter I always end the call by telling her I love her. None of us ever know when we will have that last conversation.

BRIAN—2 February 2005

Brian was a bit of a whim. It was a Friday night and I sat with the local weekly paper on my lap.

I decided that I would amuse myself with a quick look at the telephone dating page. I can't remember exactly what his advertisement said but I decided that I would ring and listen to his message. His voice was pleasant enough and he said that although he didn't look like Phil Mitchell he had similar hair or lack of it. I decided to be witty and leave him a message. I gave details of myself and said that I didn't look like Sharon Watts. The plus side of this was that I wouldn't sleep with his brother if he had one!

Next day he rang back and suddenly, in the middle of our chat, he said "Are you a size 12?" This, obviously, meant a great deal to him. I figured that maybe his ex-wife had left all her size 12 dresses behind and he didn't fancy taking them to Oxfam or perhaps he was a cross-dresser looking to extend his/her wardrobe. I told him that I was a size 16 and I could tell, by the ensuing silence, that this was not to his liking.

I then decided to get personal, after all he had. I waited ten seconds and then asked him what size it was. "What size is what?" he demanded. "Well what do you think I mean?" I said sweetly.

Brian was not a happy bunny and he put the 'phone down on me. I only wanted to know the size of his ego but I think I had already guessed it. So, Rose West if the prison food is not to your liking, and you are down to a size 12, 'phone Brian. You are just the sort of trophy babe he wants on his arm.

COLD—22 February 2005

I remember standing at the foot of the Eiffel Tower getting colder by the second. The snow was the first that Paris had seen for quite some time. The freezing fog was indescribable. My coat, instead of protecting me, seemed to freeze in unison with the fog. I can remember thinking that I had never felt colder.

My travelling companion and I soon made our way to a warm café and ordered hot chocolate. I am sure that even polar bears were ordering jackets from the Damart catalogue. Goodness knows how many jumpers my daughter would be wearing if the weather was similar in the UK. When she feels the cold she wears layers of jumpers. I think the normal count is five but, as in everything, there are exceptions to the rule.

Saturday nights out, which generally start on Thursday at around 10.30 pm, are the exception. On Thursday-Saturday nights it seems that my daughter is never cold. She goes out wearing a very skimpy, wispy top with no sleeves and very little front. This is worn with a skirt that is about ten inches in length. She wears extremely high-heeled boots so I suppose I should be pleased that her ankles are warm. How she walks in these boots I do not know.

I suggest wearing a coat but apparently that would not be cool which is exactly what she is going to be after stepping outside the front door. She says she doesn't feel cold, but I don't think it's anything to do with the climate. I think it's called putting the goods on display. How do I know? Well I was young once. I travelled back from Lyme Regis to Taunton on a 650cc Norton motorbike wearing only a crash helmet and a size 10 bikini. As with all young people, I never contemplated a crash or what would have happened to my skin if I had been thrown off. So, it seems that my daughter not wearing a coat is hereditary.

I once described to her the ladies cloakroom at a nightclub. There's one girl the worse for wear on the verge of being sick. There is another who has just seen the man of her dreams being swept off his feet by someone else. There's the girl who is depressed. She has just cultivated a large spot on her chin which she thinks will ruin her evening. In an effort to ignore the breakout she has downed too many cocktails which only fuels her depression. There is also the female who has just "landed a catch" and whose over-confidence acts as an emetic for girl number 1. She lurches forward but doesn't quite manage to throw up in the toilet. I'm sure the cleaner who starts at an unearthly hour on a Sunday will be delighted about that! My daughter was surprised at the accuracy of my description but some things just never change.

My daughter's Saturday night generally ends with a kebab or some fast food containing dill pickles. You can always see the results of Thurs/Fri/Saturday nights at the taxi ranks. Pools of vomit and dill pickles. I don't know why the fast food outlets don't declare a National Dill Pickle Day—they could then visit the local taxi ranks and litter the pavement with pickles. This would save a lot of time and effort on the part of our young people—you know cut out the middle man.

FROGS—June 2005

Is there a plethora of frogs in the West Country? Do idiots come in threes? These were my thoughts when I reviewed the men in the Dating Agency that I had joined. No doubt their thoughts of me ran on similar lines. The advert for the Agency was next to one offering wooden off cuts for 10 pence a metre. Was someone trying to tell me something?

I was interviewed by the guy who ran the Agency and felt very much on display. I guess I must have passed as I was accepted as a member. Looking back, I think that anyone with sufficient cash to join would have been accepted. The Agency man telephoned you and gave you details of your victim (sorry, date). It was then up to you whether you wanted to go ahead with the date and then your telephone number was given to that person. I was happy with this as I am ex-directory so they had no idea where you lived.

The one thing that I stressed was I wanted some intelligent conversation. Looks were not important but banter was. The following day, the Agency man gave me details of George. He was in his late fifties and had never married. He was employed by a prestigious local company and apparently had "a City and Guilds in something". It reminded me of Maureen Lipman and the old British Telecom advert "ooh, he's got an ology". Was he on the Board? Did he have shares in the Company? All this and more was racing through my mind. The answers to both these questions was "no"—he was the maintenance man. Nothing wrong with that. I have a cousin who went to Grammar School and then became a milkman. He always said he was the well-educated milkman in Taunton.

It was a hectic week-end and I was not able to get back to George until Sunday evening. I telephoned and introduced myself. I apologised for not being able to get back to him sooner. He had left his message on Friday evening. He obviously expected his call to be answered pronto. He said, peevishly, "I did leave that message on Friday". I apologised again whilst making a mental note not to do so for a third time. There was a long silence and then said "Well, I'm working on my computer at the moment". Was I meant to be impressed or chastened? Silence again. Then, unexpectedly, he said "Go on then dear". I've never been too fond of the word dear—it strikes me as the sort of word Dr Crippen would have used as he was poisoning his wife. "What?" I said. "Ask me anything you want and I'll tell you all about myself". I told George plainly and sweetly that I felt that I already knew enough about him to make a decision and that was to thank him for his interest but decline a date. It had happened again, another romance over before it had begun.

Two years later he made the headlines by marrying a Thai lady (much younger, of course) who he had met over the Internet. Maybe when he e-mailed her and said "jump" she e-mailed back to ask "how high". In my opinion, I had a lucky escape!

Once upon a time in a land not that far away a beautiful, independent, self-assured Princess happened upon a frog as she sat contemplating ecological issues on the shores of an unpolluted pond in a verdant meadow near her castle. The frog hopped into the Princess's lap and said "Elegant lady, I was once a handsome Prince until an evil witch cast a spell upon me. One kiss from you, however, and I will turn back into the dapper young Prince that I am and then, my sweet, we can marry and set up housekeeping in your castle where you can prepare my meals, clean my clothes, bear my children and forever feel grateful and happy doing so". That night, as the Princess dined sumptuously on a repast of pan-fried frog's legs in a white wine and onion sauce, she chuckled and thought to herself "I don't bloody think so!"

Did you hear about the old lady who decided she wanted a pet? She went to the pet shop and looked first at the kittens, and then she looked at the puppies. She didn't like the look of any of them. She then viewed the the birds and wasn't struck by them either. As she was leaving the shop a tiny frog spoke to her. He told her that she would not be disappointed with him if she bought him. He was a reasonable price and she decided she would buy him. She put him on the front seat of her car and he then said "Little old lady, please give me a kiss and you will receive a wonderful surprise". There was no one around so she kissed him and he turned into a handsome young man who kissed her very passionately. What did the old lady turn into? Well it was the nearest Holiday Inn she could find!

EXFOLIATION—1 July 2005

Old age (which I am rapidly approaching) does not come alone. It brings its own ups and downs. My feet were suffering. As usual, in the summer time, I let my feet spread in toe-post sandals. The skin at the base of my heels was hard and unattractive. I had a few minutes to spare so I sauntered into the Body Shop.

I asked the assistant what she would recommend. She smiled benignly and said "Oh, you wish to exfoliate". Did I? Well it was a nice posh word but something told me that exfoliation was going to cost me far more than a quick rub with a pumice stone. Ho hum.

FAIR—1 August 2005

We all have our own ideas about fairness. Because I lived most of my life feeling that I was a victim, my idea of fairness was distorted.

When I took up residence in my New Single Me Flat, I decided that I needed to go to the Old Matrimonial Home and reclaim that which was mine. I was always aware that whatever I took from my husband, I also took from my daughter, so I tempered my requests. One thing we had, in abundance, was a well-equipped kitchen. Wedding presents, gifts in later years and kitchenware that had belonged to my Mother, meant overflowing cupboards.

Having been a legal secretary I still had, 25 years on, our wedding gift list—how sad is that? It helped us to be fair to each other. Obviously, items bought whilst we were together had to be negotiable. We almost completed this task amicably—well almost. We got to the cupboard containing cut glass, jointly bought. He said "I'll let you have the champagne flutes but I'll keep the jugs". I went from simmering to boiling, but still managed not to open the motormouth. He could see that I wasn't happy and said "Well, let's put them to one side and carry on with the rest". We both knew this was going to be a bone of contention.

We carried on and dealt with everything else fairly. Again, he said "I'll let you have the champagne flutes and I'll keep the jugs, I think that's fair". The original Mrs Motormouth would have gone ballistic—but I was learning. I managed to keep my voice low and said "Fair—well let's see, you have a double electric oven with a gas hob, a microwave, a washing machine, a fridge, a freezer and a dishwasher". My eyes were flashing wildly. He then said dejectedly, "I'll wrap them shall I"? "I said "Yes".

It was several years later that I was forced, by my conscience, to realise that I did not treat him fairly throughout our life together. I was lucky to get the jugs. I was the one who called 'time' on our marriage and he may well have said "How fair is that"?

SUPERMARKETS—11 November 2005

Grocery shopping trips are only exciting to someone who has not had to do this throughout the years. Supermarkets seem to contain every kind of social misfit that you can imagine. I include myself in this motley crew. A solitary child starts wailing and you wonder if this is the signal for every other child in the store to join in. Does it work a little bit like the "twilight bark" in 101 Dalmatians? Mothers get exasperated and all the dogma they have learnt from Dr Spock goes out of the window and they start to scream abuse at the over-tired child.

You are drawn to the special offer—buy two jars of Maxwell House coffee and get the second half price. This spurs you on with renewed vigour. Suddenly, the woman who is chatting aimlessly to her less than thrilled friend takes the last two off the shelf. You are torn between stamping your foot to grappling with this woman for possession of "the treasure". You remind yourself that you are an adult and that possession is nine points of the law. Having drawn breath you also see that she is toned and looking very fit. You draw yourself up to your full height, smile through gritted teeth and retire to the next aisle.

I went to Sainsbury's this morning, committed to getting everything on my list. I get my trolley and take a deep breath. I wonder what the dance looks like from the air. Women, some very weary, joining in an intricate uncorreographed ballet. I stop at the fruit and 'veg' and pay homage to the five a day. Another shopper is having difficulty in deciding which pre-packed mushrooms she should buy. I pick up a pack but can feel the intensity in her. Has she scrutinised them already or have I just deprived her of that pleasure? I feel that I should hand her a brown paper bag, supplied for loose mushrooms, in case she hyperventilates. Maybe I should make that two bags in case the first bag is not up to her standard.

I get everything on my list and then try and sneak up on the reduced shelves. When I was with He Who Will Never Be Forgotten, he used to come home with a cut-price curry and several delicious pies. Whenever I try to get a bargain there are 44 plain economy yoghurts, which I am happy to ignore.

Today, apart from one article, nothing beckons to me even at a knock-down price. The one article is something I will never need. It is a Clear Blue pregnancy test. I imagine it must have a sell-by date? I would never consider buying something as important as this at a reduced price. I mean, imagine drawing a blank and heaving a big sigh of relief only to discover a few months later that it should have shown positive. I am told by a friend that you can also get them for £1 in Poundland. Caveat emptor—let the buyer beware!

SOD'S LAW—January 2006

"Let a smile be your umbrella"—George Carlin (37)

The law, according to sod, is known to all of us. If you are early the bus is late. If you are on time the bus won't be. If you are ten seconds late the bus will have left. There is always a change of drivers when it is wet and/or freezing. Most drivers will close their doors, use their mobile 'phone or have a good old natter with each other.

My worst experience was getting drenched during a change-over and then being told the driver couldn't change a £10 note. He suggested I change it in a nearby shop and said he would be there for a few minutes. I hastened into Clintons and looked for something that would not cause too much financial damage to my purse. I grabbed a postcard of a pig—my friend Margaret collects anything porcine. I decided to send it to her when next on holiday rather than the usual sea and sand offering.

There were two women in the queue, one of whom was putting her change away. She must have sensed my urgency and decided to engage the assistant in a chat about this and that. My blood pressure was rising and my pupils were dilated. I wondered if a judge and jury would accept a plea of justifiable homicide when I heard the grating of gears.

The bus was pulling out and the driver had a maniacal grin plastered on his face. Mentally I think he was saying "Happy New Year". He could hardly contain his enjoyment. My unprintable thoughts about his benevolence were lost in the condensation and depression that only an early January day can bring.

ANN SUMMERS WINDOW 19 April 2006

"At it like rabbits baby" says the sign on the window. It was strategically placed at a height ideal for an intelligent five year old to read. I can almost hear a child say "At what Mummy"?

Sex is good, no sex is great and I'm not a prude but the sign is out of order. Did you see the recent display of see-through boxer shorts and balcony Y fronts? No, nor did I. Any woman that tells you we're regarded as equal to men should have a look at Ann Summers' window today. Apparently, they do sell firemen and police uniforms but they never appear in the window. Do they have any male mannequins? I doubt it.

In the Inquest papers for my Grandmother there is a statement that Grandma had 17 children. Some were stillborn or died shortly after birth. There were two sets of twins but only one set prospered. Someone commented that my Grandma was a popular lady but I have to say that would only have been with my Grandfather. She was either in bed having them or making them. I would also bet (and my Grandfather would not have approved of that!) that she never had to diet or dress provocatively to tempt him. Just imagine how many children she might have had if she did!

ANN SUMMERS WINDOW—Yet again—16 May 2013

"I have yet to hear a man ask for advice on how to combine marriage and a career" Gloria Steinem (38)

Nothing much changes does it? Since I wrote my piece on this subject in April 2006, I still check out this window. Part of the reason for this is that it is very near the bus stop and, as an optimist; I want to see the see-through boxer shorts and balcony Y fronts. They have still not appeared.

In recent times they had an advert which said "any way you want me" and also a display of lacy handcuffs which were advertised as being "brand spanking new". So who do we thank for this? I have not read the book "Fifty Shades of Grey" but I know many, many women who have. Personally, I think women already have a tough deal and such adverts, in my opinion, don't make a woman's lot easier.

We are encouraged to have a career whilst still managing the housework and children. No doubt Jo Frost, the childcare expert would be able to help us with that. The media tells us that we should be a Yummy Mummy. Wikipedia says that this is a slang term used in the UK to describe young, attractive and wealthy mothers.

In 2008 it was reported that celebrity Yummy Mummies were contributing to levels of depression in young mothers making new mothers feel "saggy, baggy and depressed" about their own bodies. What we fail to see is the army of people behind these YMs. Not many of them change nappies or cook meals and never have to worry about the cost of a personal trainer. They can afford the expensive food which keeps their figures trim. So should we be concerned that we don't measure up to their standards? How can we be the Yummy Mummy dropping off Arabella and Tarquin at ballet and martial arts classes? Apparently, we should have managed a full day's work before this whilst arriving at the dropping off points with perfect make-up and hair. Prior to this we should have prepared the evening meal, made from scratch with all of the 5 a day contents. We should also have managed the ironing and the housework.

I'm old now and a little wiser so this stuff does not apply to me. To summarise, potential YMs should be Jo Frost with the children, Nigella Lawson in the kitchen and up for anything with their man in the bedroom. Does this make me want to read "Fifty Shades of Grey"? No I am too knackered and I've gone a whiter shade of pale. Kinky sex—nah I'd settle for 8 solid hours of sleep!

BLISS IN CORNWALL—5 June 2006

Sensible people acknowledge when they are tired. They don't try to "climb every mountain". They rest, recuperate and live to fight another day. I had reached a certain degree of "tiredness" and so headed off for three days in a lovely Cornish resort. I am drawn there partly because my forefathers were Cornish and partly for the laid back culture which seems to exist.

I really enjoyed my stay because I went expecting to do just that. I caught the bus to re-visit a village which was dear to my heart. Where else could you find a shop which opened at 10 am with a note on the door saying "back in five minutes" at 10.20? Polperro was much as I remembered it 40 years ago, except the Post Office had gone and you can't drive through the village any more. People don't seem to want to walk these days and many travel on the horse driven vehicles that are, no doubt, profitable for their owners.

I arrived early in the morning and decided to go window shopping. That was not easy. Some of the windows had the displayed goods ruined by the sun. Some had been ruined by the sun of several summers. The hideous gifts, to take home for people you don't really like, looked pale and uninviting. Price tickets had faded away with time. Luckily I don't have odious family members to buy for. On my way out of the village I stopped to look in the window of "Ye Olde Cornish fudge shop". I decided against taking some back for my work colleagues. I felt it would be churlish of me to ask the assistant to carbon date the fudge. My colleagues, like my family, are not odious.

I arrived back at the bus stop just in time to see forty or so French students who had been spewed out from a coach. Their raucous exchanges shattered the calm and serene Cornish idyll.

Once back "at base camp" I decided to have a pint in "Ye Olde Fisherman". The price was extortionate. I wondered if I was, in fact, supporting "Many Generations of Ye Olde Family" of "Ye

Olde Fisherman". The place had been run down—there was little attempt to dust or sweep the floor. Perhaps they thought it added to the authenticity. However, the pumps on the bar looked slightly more cared for. I decided that I had to trust the publican and God on the matter of hygiene.

There were sandwiches in a cabinet, which the old British Rail would have been proud of. They curled at the edges, had indistinct fillings and were priced astronomically. My hunger waned. A further half pint of "Ye Olde Cornish Ale" and I would be on my way. I was obviously not going to get a look at "Ye Olde Fisherman" but there was a distinct odour. I felt sure that he was not very far away. He was probably in the back bar laughing maniacally as he counted yesterday's takings.

I spent my last day watching the river traffic. Doing nothing can be extremely soothing to the soul as well as to the mind and body. I will go back later in the year to gather what shards of peace and serenity that remain. I shall clutch them tightly to me as Cornwall has, yet again, worked its magic and captured my heart.

DOWNSIZING—10 July 2006

A friend rang last night to apologise for not coming over to see me. She said "We are one car down at the moment" and I said "Me too". Some people find it hard to imagine life without a car. I found it hard at first but it certainly helped me to develop muscles through carrying shopping. If I don't want to carry it, then I can shop on the Net and, occasionally, my ex-husband takes me to Tesco if he is going there to shop.

When I downsized my life from us to me—I gave up many material things. My shopping trolley with a few bits and pieces was all I took. Well, come on, I couldn't play the part of the victim if I had taken any luxury items! I gradually settled into my new accommodation and some familiar items trickled from the Old Matrimonial Home to the New Single Me Flat.

A friend complained that she had been running the hot water tap in the kitchen for ages but the water was still cold. I said "That's because the immersion heater's not on"—she looked puzzled. She had never lived anywhere where this had been an option. I didn't have a hoover for quite some time but a dustpan and brush did an admirable job and I needed the exercise.

Eventually I was able, with the help of a Building Society, to buy a small, one bedroom house. He Who Will Never Be Forgotten was in my life by then and was keen to see it. I said we could visit over the weekend but that Friday evening was mine and mine alone. Yes, I felt proud. I walked in and was immediately grateful that Trudy, the previous owner, had left the net curtains and carpets. I had a single bed, a second-hand television and a table.

What on earth would I fill this house with? I went to a second-hand dealer to get a fridge/freezer, cooker, washing machine, tumble drier and a chair for the lounge. I picked them out quickly and asked them to deliver. Mary, the owner said "Well you certainly don't take long to make decisions". I explained that previously I had had matching everything but it didn't give me any great joy. All I wanted now was stuff that worked.

> *"You can't have everything—after all where would you put it? Steven Wright (39)*

HAIRDRESSERS—2 August 2006

Where would we be without our hairdresser? A good one is worth her weight in Kirby grips—now that really dates me! Mine sees me at my worst—well with the exception of my gynaecologist.

When I was 24, eons ago, I had my hair, which touched my waist, cut to shoulder length. It was so thick and took an age to wash and dry. The other women in the salon were silenced as my locks fell to the ground. Why was I having it cut? Because someone told me that as I was over 21 I would have to start wearing my hair up. Why did I listen? Who knows? At one salon, I always seemed to be the first customer of the morning and it coincided with the hairdresser/owner opening the post. Very often, it seemed, the contents were not to her liking and boy did my scalp suffer!

I suppose I've had four or five different hairdressers—I'm not a fan of spending too much time in salons. Shellie was my hairdresser for over ten years. She was superb and I am sad at leaving her. She has been so much more than just a hairdresser. She saw me through some life-changing experiences and updated my style when needed. I never looked into a mirror to check—I knew I could rely on her to make my hair look good. In the office, I would announce that tomorrow was "tart red day". This meant that I would be having my hair cut and coloured. Shellie did take issue with the "tart red"—she said it was teak. So what's in a name?

Because Shellie has moved, I went elsewhere last week. A superb cut and a lighter colour—so "tart red" is, after quite some time, on its way out. I also bought a little pot of "Fudge hair shaper". I'm not too sure if I will get on with it. A work colleague also uses and recommends this. She tells me that it is an Australian product—but one thing's for sure, I won't be using it down under!

Did you hear about the woman who asked her hairdresser to cut one side above the ear, the other side below and could she make the fringe uneven? She was incensed and protested—"I can't do that". The customer said "Well you managed it last time love".

What about the guy who asked his hairdresser to give him a Brad Pitt style haircut? After some fast and furious cutting the customer said angrily, "Brad Pitt doesn't have his hair cut like that". The barber replied "Well he would if he came here".

THE PC SYNDROME—10 April 2012

A kind of hush came over the salon as she walked in. There was an air of suspicion and I was not surprised to hear in a whisper that she had, apparently, upset nearly everyone in the salon because of her attitude. This woman was a serious sucker of lemons— either that or she was imitating a cat's bottom with her lips. I got the impression that she thought she should really be attending a better class salon or that she should be paid for her patronage.

My hairdresser, an experienced woman of salons, if not the world, knows exactly how to handle her. When the criticisms come, as they surely do, Lisa knows that this is not due to any error on her part. Last week, "lemon lips" complained about the lack of a gown—Lisa patiently explained that the rubber cape would make sure that no water would touch her. She insisted on a gown as "its part of the whole experience". She obviously thought a trip to the hairdressers was much more of an occasion than I did. Lisa, patiently, gave her a gown but then she moaned that it didn't have arms. One could almost forgive her that attitude as it was mildly entertaining but I thought her demonstration of how her fringe should be blow dried was a little too much. If she was that good why bother with a salon at all? Throughout all of this, Lisa smiled and kept her inner thoughts well hidden. She soared in my estimation.

In the client's defence, I have to say that she is one of many who suffer from the PC syndrome. More and more people seem to be going down with it. Antibiotics are ineffective and there is no operation that will cure it. The only remedy is for the sufferer to remove it themselves and not many of them try. They prefer to think that it is the rest of humanity that is out of kilter. The PC syndrome is simply, but painfully, having a pine cone up your arse. Lady Muck is the only woman I know who can have her nose in the air whilst having her head up her arse. The medical term for this is Rectal Cranial Inversion. Presumably she is searching for the illusive pine cone.

Some people are so badly affected that they can't be civil to anyone. Men, as well as women, can be struck down with this uncomfortable malaise. I was hearing, recently, of a flight being cancelled at a well known airport. The desk clerk was dealing with a long line of anxious people who had places to see and people to meet. Suddenly, right from the back of the queue came a man who brushed past all the other patient travellers. He demanded to be put on the next available flight. The clerk asked him to wait in line with the others and assured him that she was doing the best she could. He drew himself up to his full height and said, in a very loud voice, "Do you know who I am?" The clerk put down her pen and reached for the microphone. She announced "This is Gate 8; we have a gentleman here who is about 5' 10" tall, aged between 55 to 65. He doesn't know who he is. If anyone can help him then please hurry to Gate 8." He was incandescent with rage and hissed at the clerk "F..k you!" She smiled serenely as she replied "Well you'll have to get in line for that too."

I heard another tale of a very patient check-in clerk who was being unfairly berated by an angry passenger. The next person she served was amazed by her longstanding sufferance for the former traveller. The girl smiled sweetly and said "Yes, he is going to New York but his luggage is going to Sydney".

TECHNOLOGY—20 August 2006

I am really proud of myself—tired but proud. I've had a lie-down and recouped my energy. I haven't scaled Mount Everest but it was nearly as challenging—I sent my first text message

Technology and I have a troubled past and I think we view each other with mistrust. There was a time when I handled technology quite well. This was when you had to wind up the gramophone and pat that little terrier on the head. I exaggerate—I did, at the age of 13, have a second-hand Dansette record player. It had an automatic turntable but you had the place the stylus on the record itself. Scary stuff!

I don't like techno babble 'cos it's a foreign language to me. I've always thought that megahertz happened when you fell for the wrong man and megabytes were what you got when you stood on the cat's tail. To me an iPod sounds like a genetically modified vegetable and MP3 is surely part of the postcode for a northern town or city.

However, I can't afford to be ignorant of the 21st century. So, today, I sent that text message. It was not a long message owing to the fact that I managed to delete it several times before actually sending it. I e-mailed my Daughter, she being the Principal of the Expert School in Texting. The little so-and-so, not realising that this was a momentous event in the life of Mummy, didn't send a reply but did confirm over the 'phone later that she had received it. I've decided that I shall pluck up courage and send another text next year.

I recently heard of another lady's struggle with technology—she told a friend that she could not buy a set top box as her television wasn't wide enough!

BEING IN CONTROL—9 September 2006

Five years ago I decided to go abroad on my own for a week. I would have liked my significant other to accompany me but he was still being a "victim" and a nice holiday in a warm climate didn't quite fit in with that.

I had never flown solo before and I'm not a fan of air travel. On a bad day I'm not a fan of any travel! I was flying from Gatwick, so I had to book an overnight hotel in darkest Sussex. The TV didn't work and the radiators, which could not be regulated, were set on scorcheo! After a short, sweaty catnap I drank a small cup of bitter coffee. At what seemed to be a very unreasonable hour, I was transported to the airport.

As I went down the tunnel ready to board the plane, I kept asking myself what I was doing. It was a real battle with the Inner Child who was so-o-o scared. The adult me had to triumph over the Child if the holiday was to happen. I had to speak quite authoratively to her. My Doctor had prescribed 6 Valium tablets and one of those crunched up and swallowed with a can of Stella Artois seemed to do the trick. I sat in my seat and took a deep breath,

The lady next to me was wearing a lovely perfume. I commented on this and we got talking. She realised that I was apprehensive and I admitted that take-off bothered me. I feel that if you voice your fears they lose some of their power. Anyway, take-off is imminent hence more deep breaths from me and a kind offer from her. She says "Would you like to hold my hand?" In an effort to ignore the feeling of the plane's thrust, I said "You're a very attractive woman, but no thanks". We both laugh and more of my fear is reduced.

I have this theory that the nearer the ground you are the better the chance of survival. This is probably untrue but I am happy in my ignorance. It helps me to land reasonably calmly.

When the stewardess does the safety patter (which must be so boring for them) I have an urge to say "Come on love, if anything goes wrong we're going to die". I think if I ever did say it, I would then panic and someone would have to slap my face. Mass hysteria might then kick in and the face slapping queue could lengthen. Something to do with stating the obvious.

A colleague tells me that she has made a conscious decision never to fly again. She asks me how I can be in control if I have taken my Valium cocktail. I look at her incredulously. The only being in control when you are up there is God. I try to imagine that God is holding the plane in His hand and pray that the pilot has not been to an all-night party.

I had a wonderful holiday and met many interesting people. I land back at Gatwick at 4.30 on a Friday afternoon. My coach left for Heathrow and I experienced all the delights of rush hour. It seemed to take as long to get from Gatwick to Heathrow as it did to fly back to the UK.

I needed to find which coach would take me back to the West Country. I found the office which said "Tickets and Enquiries" for National Express coaches. I was about to meet a very bored and boring person called "Don't know and don't wanna know". You may think you haven't met her/him but you will have in some walk of life. I queued; the British can always be relied upon to make an orderly queue of one. I didn't realise, when DKandDWK shouted "next" with murder in her eyes, that I was not going to get customer service of any description. "What stand number do I need for Taunton in Somerset?" I asked politely. She drew herself up and tensed her muscles ready for her reply. She regarded me over the top of her glasses. She looked at me much as one would on finding a Christmas sprout behind the fridge at the end of February. She was triumphant in declaring "I have no idea" and then shouted "next". She will never know how close this old sprout came to decking her!

The second time I flew alone I had to change in Amsterdam for Johannesburg. I had the aisle seat. A couple came to claim their seats and immediately the woman started to panic. She said she would have to speak to the stewardess as she had to have an aisle seat so that she could "get out". Fears are often irrational but I decided not to ask her how she intended "getting out" while we were flying at a zillion feet. I tell her that she can have my seat and I move to the window. Let's face it, I am not like her—I am petrified no matter where I sit!

HAMSTER—5 November 2006

It's amazing how meeting up with an old work colleague can bring back such memories. In the mid '60s I worked as a shorthand typist for a local clothing manufacturer. The Company is long gone now, but I well remember the new Manager who turned work into hard labour and fostered hostility between management and staff. We worked in blocks of four, a section Manager, an order clerk, filing clerk and shorthand typist. It was a busy office and it worked well.

The new Manager decided that we should all sit in rows and face his desk. If you wanted to leave the room you had to raise your arm and then get permission. I was lucky; at least I didn't have a weak bladder! Because of restrictive rules, my job left me feeling rather like a Bond cocktail—shaken but not stirred. At times it resembled a Disney film, at others, Psycho.

Most of my colleagues were good people. The new Manager enjoyed having meetings about meetings and was full of office-speak. Who was he trying to impress—and did I really care?

We were constantly encouraged to look for short cuts. I did think that my suggestions (unvoiced, of course) to improve time management and production were novel but possible. Instead of having to raise your arm to ask permission for a wee we could all have been catheterised and then have a central gully which the waste could be directed in a suitable gathering chamber. We could also have fitted everyone with a gastric feeding tube—this would have ruled out visiting the excellent canteen we had. This could then have been shut down and more savings made. It would also negate the need for a lunch hour.

Perhaps the dreaded Manager should have fitted us with earpieces so that his carefully selected words could spur us onwards to our ultimate goal, this being to worship at the shrine of the end of month statistics. If all the staff had been neutered then they would not have had to take leave in the school holidays. Working as we did generated a lot of stress.

> *"I thought I saw the light at the end of the tunnel but it was some b . . . . d with a torch bringing me more work"*—David Brent (40)

TAFFY—January 2007

"A Welsh man prays on his knees on a Sunday and on his friends the rest of the week." (41) Anon. From the guardian.com in their article "Don't be so snobby about Wales".

We met on the Internet and e-mailed each other every day, sometimes twice a day. His advertisement said "I'm genuine, I hope you are too". Priceless, absolutely priceless. I'm sure that he is genuine, possibly even once a day but only before he gets out of bed. After a few weeks he gave me his telephone number and from then on we took it in turns to call. One day in December he phoned me five times, always saying "Hi gorgeous".

When you are of a certain age, not good looking or slender you are vulnerable. No friends of mine had met him and indeed if they had they may also have fallen under his spell. That sounds as though all the faults were his and that would not be true. But, and it is a big But—I didn't deserve to be treated badly.

We never ran out of conversation and decided to meet up and spend a weekend together. It was the first of four occasions. It was a risk for both of us.

As it turned out we "clicked"—I should have remembered that dislocated joints click but I ignored the warning signs, the weaknesses, and the self indulgence and ploughed headlong into a very one-sided relationship. My need masked the warning signs that this man was definitely not for me. He could not provide the TLC that I was looking for but my need said "maybe he will give this later" how could I allow myself such self-deprecating sentiment?

Quite early on—before we actually met—I told him that I now got on well with my ex-husband. He said that he and his ex-wife also got on well and tried to help each other when they could. They had been divorced for quite some years as had I. After a further

2 weekends at my place, I suggested visiting him. He told me that there were some people in the village who weren't nice. He was the only "not nice" person I came across. Eventually, as our relationship "took off" someone in the village rang Blodwen, his ex-wife and told her of my existence. She was apparently very upset and would have no more to do with him. I commented that she must still have strong feelings for him. He admitted that in the years since they broke up she had never been out with anyone else. I was to learn later why she felt they were still an item. I spent a few days in Wales after Blodwen had been informed of my existence.

The first evening we went to a pub and there was entertainment on. The artiste was obviously half way through a sex change operation and I was unable to work out if the moustache and muscles were coming or going. He/she had a strong and pleasant voice. Whilst he/she had a break the only music that was played (and it was a long evening) was Tom Jones. I have never been a fan and that evening did nothing to change my opinion. It was quite a surreal event—so many seemingly macho men wearing far more jewellery than their partners.

Taffy and I discovered, long before we actually physically met, that we had been in the same holiday resort the previous January, literally within a few yards of each other. When forging a relationship finding coincidences, common ground seems to reaffirm that you are suited to each other. This does not just apply to romantic relationships—we are all delighted when we meet people and find out we have some mutual friends, went to the same University, or had children the same year. We long to belong. We look for these links to validate our social intercourse. Umm that word, intercourse brings me back to lover boy.

It is said that man has a brain and a penis but only enough blood supply to work one at a time. Well, fate had been doubly cruel to Taffy as neither was up to scratch. Every day was definitely out of the question and so I found myself every fourth or fifth day being "on hold" waiting to see if the little blue pill would work its magic. There was no question of any foreplay—it was "brace yourself girl this is going to be the best ten seconds of your life". Shakespeare would definitely have called this "much ado about nothing". Tenderness, closeness, cuddles—forget it—this was a one-way street.

There were definitely three of us in the relationship at all times, me, him and his ego. I got just a tad weary of hearing how many women fancied him. The fact that he could do nothing physical about it for at least four days out of seven did not seem to daunt him. Obviously, like me, all his conquests were extremely patient. He could certainly talk a good time though. What a mighty ego!

We had only been at our holiday destination for half an hour before he received a text from Sandra. I asked who she was and was told she was the last squeeze before me. She was just texting to give him her new address—how kind of her!

The rented apartment was very much to his liking and so, apparently, was the female security guard, Hester. She was very much like me in looks and height. I went shopping one morning and on my return the lovely Hester was sat in the apartment I had paid for, drinking tea with Mega Ego. I was not best pleased and I think they both gathered that. She very weakly said "So you've been shopping then". I gave her my best withering glance and thought "Yeah and so have you honey". Mighty Ego explained, after she left, that she had come to ask for a donation towards a leaving gift for a cleaner in the apartment block. What that had to do with a holiday let I'll never know. Was it just an excuse to gain entry or had he been down to the lobby to invite her up? If only his prowess had matched his intent but then I guess he would have been four stone lighter.

Later in the week, Mighty Ego asked if I was taking home a present for my ex-husband as he was looking after my cat. I said I didn't need to as I would cat-sit for him later in the year. I was stunned by his next remark. He asked if my ex would expect payment in kind. Suddenly the light bulb in my brain lit up. Taffy was still banging Blodwen! Yes, I can almost hear some males from the Valleys saying "There's tidy look you". No wonder she got annoyed when she found out about me.

Luckily she only called once a week so he was able to calculate when to take the 'luvve' pill. Did Blodwen, in some dysfunctional way, believe that the couple that sleeps together keeps together? Mighty Ego did, grudgingly admit that this was why she thought they were still an item. We were standing in the kitchen of the apartment when I challenged him on this. He thought it really odd that my ex and I didn't do the same.

I was still reeling from this revelation when he hit me with another. He said that he wanted to be honest and so was telling me that the next morning he was meeting up to have coffee with a woman he had met the previous year. I reacted in the worst way possible for him—I laughed and laughed. The sheer audacity of the man. There was an element of Brian Rix in the old Whitehall farces except Mighty Ego did not like being laughed at. He said that if I was not happy then he would not go. More laughter from me. Mega Ego was puce coloured and not at all happy.

I had lost all and every illusion I had about him. He was free to meet up with any woman he wanted. Ideally she should have been Lucretia Borgia but one can't have everything. At least I was off the Viagra Watch. Naturally the next day not a lot of chat passed between us and hey guess what—Hester also had the day off. Well, what a surprise! He returned several hours early saying that "she" had not turned up. Maybe he was going to her place for some afternoon delight and her husband had turned up unexpectedly. How very inconsiderate. Had he overdosed on Viagra and did I care? I managed to keep a straight face and resolved to spend the rest of the holiday being civil but distant. He couldn't accept that and tried on several occasions to "pull" me.

Mighty Ego had problems with the F and C words—no, not those. I mean F for faithfulness and C for couple. Exclusivity had obviously never been one of his attributes even during his two marriages. He saw himself as flamboyant, captivating and fascinating. I would describe him as flaccid, corpulent and flatulent. To be far away from home with someone who has no respect for you is not the best scenario. At the end of the holiday I felt extremely used. Oh and the final detail to add to his loveliness—he still owes me for his share of the holiday.

Afterthoughts:—He boasted that he only used a designer aftershave. I won't name it in case sales slump. What he actually smelled of was essence of skunk with a soupcon of sewer rat. You'll have noted by now my love of phrases and several spring to mind.

> For me "if you lose, don't lose the lesson"—H. Jackson Brown Jr (42)—and I won't.

> "For him its "there's no such thing as a free lunch" Milton Friedman (43).

> "There are still parts of Wales where the only concession to gaiety is a stripped shroud" Gwyn Thomas (44)

Is still banging Blodwen the reason they sing "We'll keep a welcome in the hillsides?"—Rosie

A NEW MAN?—17 April 2007

He: You look very tired darling.

She: Yeah. I feel I could sleep for a week.

He: I'll cook tea—my pasta dish is your favourite, right?

She: I love it but the kids are going to need picking up from school and there's shopping to be done as well as some hand washing, but thanks for the offer.

He: I'll leave early and go to Sainsbury's, then pick up the kids, feed them and prepare the pasta dish for us. How does that sound?

She: You are wonderful. But I haven't made a shopping list.

He: Leave that to me. I'll put the hand washing soaking in cool water and look in the cupboards, fridge and freezer and put a list together.

She: You are an absolute darling.

He: Have a nice, relaxing bath while I'm gone. Use some of the lavender bath soak. Then get into bed and try to sleep. I'll wake you at 7:30 with your supper on a tray. Then I'll give you a big cuddle so that you will know how much you mean to me. And before you say it, no the cuddle will be all that I want. I'm just such a lucky man having you as a wife.

What happens next girls?

Yes, the alarm clock wakes you—its 6 am, world war three has broken out in the kids' rooms and he is snoring loudly next to you. Welcome to the real world!

LOVE?—2 May 2007

> *Love many, trust few*
> *Always paddle your own canoe (45)—American proverb*

Who you love and how you love will depend on what you have witnessed in your childhood. Saying this, however, does not mean that you have no responsibility in this. You need to examine your parents' relationship and decide if it was good or bad and what you can learn from that.

I tell myself that it is better to be on my own than in a bad relationship. I have my own front door and control what happens in my house and in my life. In the past, when there was a man around I have cancelled out my feelings. Back then, whatever they wanted to eat was fine and I found myself cooking only that. I have watched the programmes they watched. It's like I slowly faded away, seemingly having no thoughts, opinions or feelings of my own. How can I have submerged my wants, needs and feelings and, when I have, where did they go? I buried them deep but then would get resentful and any partner would be left bewildered by my moods and non-communication.

I think the Child within me selected the worse kind of character and then I convinced myself that this is what I deserve. I remember a good friend who, on falling in love yet again, said "We share the same interests, stained glass windows and bird watching". She joined the RSPB and read avidly any information she could gather on our little feathered friends. In the thirty odd years that I had known her she had never expressed any interest in church architecture or birdies.

I recognise this dedication to the new man as I have done it myself. In the past, when a relationship has turned really toxic, I have clung on with all the proclivities of a limpet!

> "Love: a temporary insanity curable by marriage"—
> Ambrose Bierce (46).

THROWING A PITY PARTY—20 July 2007

There's nothing wrong with watching a film or listening to music that you know will make you cry. A friend says that her tears are her strength. They don't change anything but they allow you to validate your feelings.

I once went to Church four Sundays in a row and spent the entire time in silent tears. I was blessed with a Minister who had experienced severe emotional pain and when I apologised for my red eyes he said "emotions are never wrong".

Last Saturday I decided to throw a pity party for myself. There was no need to send out an invitation, I was already in attendance. I chose the film "Edward Scissorhands" for the millionth time knowing that it would trigger some tears. The light fitting in my lounge only had one spotlight working so there was plenty of doom and gloom. There has to be food at a party, so I decided to make a "woe-is-me" cake. Mix equal measures of self pity, self doubt and loathing. Allow ingredients to fester. Beat (yourself) until exhausted. Sprinkle with a handful of "nobody loves me" seeds and once cooked (or fermented in the mind) top with a bitter icing of "I'm no good at anything". Whilst waiting for the 'cake' to cool, the mantra of "fat, stupid and ugly" should be chanted, loudly.

Should there be alcohol? Perhaps sufficient to make you maudlin but not enough to anaesthetise yourself—this would defeat the object of the exercise.

When I lived in the New-Single-Me-Flat I could feel a pity party building. I had a few china ornaments which I no longer wanted. The flat across the way from me was vacant and the chap upstairs always went out on a Wednesday evening. I waited for him to leave and then had "a smashing time". There was still red-hot emotion left in me once the smashing had ended and so I beat on the wall with my hands. I felt nothing but the adult me had to tend the bruises the next day.

DEPRESSION—22 September 2007

It is upon me again, I have slipped into the abyss. In the '60s and '70s it was obvious from my diaries exactly where I was emotionally. There would be many, many entries about entertaining friends, events to attend and much burning of the candle at both ends. Then, quite abruptly, it would come. There would be page after page with no entries at all. Winston Churchill called it his "black dog".

Sure, I functioned as a machine would function but joy, laughter, fun and light heartedness had obviously hitched a ride out of my part of town. The depression would be all-encompassing. I groped my way through the days and weeks of the blackness. I tended not to see many people or attend previously enjoyed events. People who saw the happy actress and only knew the superficial me would not have been able to understand the black place that laid claim to me from time to time.

There would be, and still is, a great deal of tiredness connected to the depression. I felt/feel like a fruit whose juice had/has been extracted. Every aspect of my life suffered and it wasn't easy for my husband. He had his own share of problems. I am not finding this easy to write about—will it be cathartic? Maybe, but my main aim is to set the record straight. Depression is not for always. Catch you tomorrow?? The question marks are for me not you.

> *"Depression is a prolonged form of sadness"—Paul Besley (47)*

> *"Where there is depression, there is always hope"—Paul Besley (48)*

> *"One very depressed man once said to me some years after recovery "you were the only person who told me that one day I would get better"—Paul Besley (49)*

DEPRESSION TWO—1 October 2007

Sorry for not getting back to you sooner. It can be the nature of the beast. To be perfectly honest when I feel like this I don't want to write. I don't think I deserve the happiness that writing brings me.

Depression is wearing the same baggy and unflattering clothes day after day. They are there and you barely register putting them on. You don't remember the last time you combed your hair. When you are badly depressed you don't want to get up. You don't want to pull the curtains back to start a new day. Enthusiasm is just a word in the dictionary and joy is just a rumour that's reserved for other people.

Depression is sitting in a chair doing nothing and four hours have gone by. Depression is not wanting to answer the 'phone or the door. Simple tasks exhaust you. The day and your mood are bleak, black and bottomless. Depression is hell on earth—pure hell.

3 October 2007

I have found a website called Mixed Nuts which is very informative. 42 writers, 78 poets, 32 composers and 42 artists suffered with depression. Out of these 194 talented people, 61 spent some time in hospital or an asylum. 24 made suicide attempts and 40 committed suicide. Of the suicides only 8 were hospitalised before going on to commit the act. Of those who made suicide attempts not one went on to fulfil their original wish. So it seems that I am in an illustrious group although I am not crass enough to place my scribbled musings against any talent of theirs. If I did, then I would have to be treated for delusions of grandeur as well as depression!

TALKING OF DEPRESSION

> *Depression keeps uneasy company*
> *With language;*
> *And my Doctor, wanting words,*

Enquiries bizarrely: "How have your moods been?"
As if they were somehow detached from me
And lived in separate rooms about the House
Smiling politely each night over tea,
When asked to pass the mustard.—Natalie Hensby (50)

Neurotics build castles in the air
Psychotics dwell in them
The psychiatrist just collects the rent—Jerome Lawrence (51)

COTFORD—THE SECOND SOMERSET COUNTY ASYLUM—5 November 2007

"Nothing in life is to be feared. It is only to be understood"—Marie Curie (52)

The first County Asylum was built at Wells and by 1891 was overfull. The second Somerset County Asylum was opened at Cotford in 1897 and finally closed its doors on 5 April 1995. I can highly recommend the book "The Tone Vale Story"—A century of care, edited by David Hinton and Fred Clarke published by Rocket Publishing Co. Ltd at Bishops Lydeard.

July 1980. I came across her in Sainsburys. Her face looked very familiar and she gave me a warm smile and greeting. I knew that I had seen her before but had to be honest and ask where we had met. She leaned over in a very conspiratorial manner and whispered "Tone Vale". She got a thin smile back and we passed a few minutes talking about our families. I turned to my husband and acknowledged my lack of details on how she and I had got along and what she was "in there" for. Seeking to be helpful and supportive he would say "It was summer 1977". I had spent a total of 15 weeks "in there" as a voluntary patient with severe depression. I signed up for nine treatments of electro-convulsive therapy. My brain was blitzed and I lost many good memories. The bad ones, however, remained. Below is an extract of my diary regarding Tone Vale and the sadness that encompassed me for a great deal of my life.

Spew and spittle cover the streets of this town. Alcohol abounds and aggression rises. We try to contact other planets whilst completely mismanaging our own. But there is progress—Cotford no longer stands. The railings which kept the madness in or out depending on your view are long gone. People with epilepsy are not incarcerated there and pregnant single women get a council house now rather than being committed because they were "out of control".

I spent a good deal of my life pretending that I was ok. I ran and ran to escape from that which I carried with me all the time. I ran to ill-qualified people hoping that they would have the answer when I did not fully comprehend the question. I was like the ball in a pinball machine—I ricochet off many people and situations frantically looking for approval. I was like a whirlwind—wreaking havoc and destruction. I captured hostages who did not deserve my revenge.

I had major issues about my face. I lost some very precious people through family moves, deaths and more particularly suicide. I was frequently at Frenchay Hospital for plastic surgery procedures and whenever my Mother had a breakdown or could not cope, I was sent to live with relatives. My Father left when I was fourteen. He was working in Sheffield and coming home every other weekend and then, suddenly, he stopped coming home. I think it was three years before I saw him again

I developed asthma and allergies and, not surprisingly, depression. I had left home before I was sixteen. I lived with an Aunt but was eventually asked to leave two years later because I was just too obnoxious. Eventually I got a room at the YWCA which I could ill afford, so food became a luxury. However, like many of that era, I always seemed to have enough money for cigarettes.

My Mother would buy me a steak meal each Saturday and I could have had a new dress as well. Relatives told my Mother that I was ill—but she couldn't do emotions and so she threw money at the problem. Don't get me wrong my Mother was very able at doing her emotions; she just couldn't handle anyone else's.

My Father visited the West Country on holiday and was immediately concerned at how thin and ill I looked. He took me home to my Mother and waited outside. He said that if she said she didn't want me then he would take me to London to live with him and my Stepmother. I will always be haunted by the fact that my Mother accepted my return solely to thwart my Father. I felt like a piece of meat that you barter for.

I was not fit to work and had to wait three months for an appointment with a Dr Bailey from Tone Vale. Some good food, sleep and anti-depressants seemed to take their effect and by the time I saw him I didn't seem to need a psychiatrist. He was a man ahead of his time—whilst doing research into my past I found a statement that he made in the local paper. He said "I hope that one day we shall be able to dispense with mental hospitals as such and have something like what is now referred to as a day hospital".

I married at 21 and it was just the sort of Mills and Boon wedding my Mother wanted. In the 1970s I again suffered with crippling depression and took a catalogue of prescribed drugs. The ones that I can remember were diazepam, welldorm, librium, fluanxol, nitrazapam, stelazine, lorazepam, nardil, chlorpromazine, nobrium, molypaxin, prothiaden, temazapam, anafranil and amitriptyline. My Mother had a Masters degree in taking prescription drugs and over-the-counter pain killers, so I had a good role model. If you feel I am being vitriolic towards my Mother then you're right. Twenty nine years after her death I still want to get hold of her and shake her! But in death as in life she is unreachable. Drowning and drowned in her self-pity. I can't remember how many times she was admitted to Tone Vale but I certainly knew the layout of the place before I became a temporary resident. Mother said that this was where you should go if things get you down and good girls always listen to their Mother. I need a break maybe I should watch something light-hearted on television and take some Rennies for my indigestion. A physical symptom of re-visiting an emotional past?

COTFORD 2—December 2007

In 1977 I attempted to take my own life. I regained consciousness in Intensive Care at Musgrove Park Hospital—boy was I angry at being saved. I ripped the monitors off my chest and it took two nurses to hold me down. I screamed for oblivion and the nurses were not amused. I'm so glad of the shame that I feel writing this now. Here was someone in Intensive Care who wanted to die and all the others were in there trying to hold on to their tenuous strands of life. I headed for Tone Vale Hospital but was not sectioned. I went willingly—I thought it was my birthright to carry on not coping. I was such a nightmare.

When I decided to look life in the eye in 1997, I sent for the Inquest papers on my Grandma and Mother. I would face the truth no matter what. I saw myself as a victim but knew that I had made victims of others. I applied for copies of the medical records on me during the 1970's. With the Access to Health Records Act 1990 you can apply for copies of medical records but only those since 1990. It is up to the powers that be as to whether you get copies of any earlier papers. It is not an automatic right—permission can be refused if it is thought to be detrimental to the patient.

All the old records from Tone Vale had gone to Avalon Somerset NHS in Bridgwater. I spoke to a lady who said that it was doubtful that papers from 20 years earlier would still be in existence. I told her that I knew they were there—don't ask how but I knew. Much time went by and I telephoned several times to remind them to keep searching. I had not come this far to be thwarted. They arrived in time for New Year 1998. To say they were humbling is an understatement.

What an attention seeking individual I was—I argued, stormed about and left without permission and walked home in the early hours. Tone Vale was too safe a place for me to hide and not deal with my problems. I was such a rebel—the nursing staff had a hard time with me. Dr Frank Manning was my psychiatrist—he was a super character and took no manure from me. He and I sparred verbally. I signed up for three lots of ECT—I would have had a head transplant—anything rather than suffering the emotional pain I was in. I felt cheated that the ECT had no effect on my feelings. I signed up for six more and had them. Apart from losing some good memories and suffering headaches nothing changed.

I met some characters—there was "Lauren", a young apathetic girl. She showed me a letter she had received from her Father. It spoke of coming to see her and of his love and concern for her. My Father had no idea where I was and I sure as hell didn't want him to know. I would not have risked his ire. I envied her; at least I did until I looked at her face. Lauren's father had sexually abused her from a very young age and she had told no one before. Somehow it's a cockeyed world when the abuser is free and the abused is in a mental health institution. I alerted a nurse and her father's visit was refused.

I could write a book just on the people I met there. Those that had become institutionalised walked with shuffling steps, heads bent down, and no eye contact. Were those inmates distraught when care in the community was introduced?

You had to ask for the bathplug when you wanted a bath. The toilets didn't lock in case someone strung themselves up. It was compulsory to attend occupational therapy each afternoon—I was none too thrilled about that. I covered a dish with small ceramic tiles which I gave to my Mother—I certainly never wanted to see it again.

Depressives form an alliance; we all gave each other permission not to smile. I also hated group therapy and repeatedly walked out when family life was discussed. Labelling me as an attention seeker was a very polite description. I was given sedation at night to sleep but on several occasions I would wake for a cigarette at one or two in the morning and the night staff would give me some more "medication". In fact they were vitamin C tablets. I may have been depressed but I surely never got a cold whilst I was a resident!

On my discharge I went to see a Disablement Resettlement Officer. He told me he could get me a part-time job packing butter as I was not to have any stress. I told him that packaging butter and not using my brain at all would make me very stressed. I never did register as disabled. I was not head sore, I was heart sore.

COTFORD 3—20 December 2007

A suicide occurs every 82 minutes in the UK. Presumably this figure does not include open verdicts passed at Inquests. Suicide was not decriminalised in the UK until 1961. Until that time your estate could have been forfeited for this offence. This would have been a double whammy for those left behind. It is said that a suicide victim puts his psychological skeleton in the emotional closet of the relatives he/she leaves behind.

I do not agree with the open verdicts that were recorded for my Grandmother and Mother. Grandma did not leave any note but all the facts point to suicide. The verdict for my Mother was unbelievable. Are Coroners too concerned with the suicide figures? I quote the parents of a young man, "they said the Coroner gave open verdicts because it was less upsetting for the families. As if anything could have upset us more than losing our son".

When I finally left Tone Vale I was quite open about my short residence there. Interviews for jobs ended abruptly when Tone Vale was mentioned. Prejudice abounds and is as rife today as ever. If you see someone with a plaster cast on their leg then you know that person has been in some pain even though you may never have broken a leg yourself. Mankind is not so benevolent when it comes to mental illness. Do we think that we might catch it from someone? Should all those who have been afflicted with depression wear black armbands and would we be surprised to see how many armbands there are?

I recently let a former work colleague read my full account—he was a man with physical disabilities himself, but boy did I make an error of judgment. He looked at me as though he had never known me and I sat there feeling that I had never really known him. His look made me feel ashamed and that makes me angry. My battle scars are part of my psyche. I would not want to go through those sad times again but as Nietzsche said "that which does not kill us makes us stronger".

Cotford St Luke is now a fashionable place to live but the past is not quite buried and perhaps it never should be. On my return from a weekend away in North Devon the bus called at Cotford and the main entrance building still stands. Tears welled in my eyes as I thought of the people I encountered and the sadness that I felt and then I remembered another saying. "The past is a foreign country—they do things differently there" (53) I don't despise the past because it has brought me to where I am now.

CORNWALL REVISITED—22 December 2007

> *"For the millions of us who live glued to computer keyboards at work and TV monitors at home, food may be more than entertainment. It may be the only sensual experience left". Barbara Ehrenreich—(54)*

> *"Food is the most primitive form of comfort". Sheila Graham (55)*

I am fast becoming a creature of habit. I am not sure if this is due to age or whether it's just that I know what I want. So I arrive again in the place that has given me serenity and a sense of belonging. Rather than eat at the Hotel, which I generally do, I decided to try somewhere new. The outside of the hostelry looked cared for and attractive. I entered and ordered a pint of Stella (God bless the amber nectar!) I then asked if I could put the price of the pint on my Debit Card when I ordered my lunch. The gentleman behind the bar said they would only take cash or a cheque. I knew where my cheque book was and it wasn't in my handbag. I can't remember the last time I wrote a cheque. The circumstances for payment were kind of thrown down as a challenge. I was hungry and not in the mood to take issue with this. I looked at the menu and then in my purse and I could afford a meal and a further half pint of Stella to go with it.

The Landlord then pointed out the various boards detailing "special dishes". I noticed that the whole place seemed to have lots of boards and notices. Someone was very fond of coloured marker pens and CAPITALS. My money (in the form of a cheque, of course) was on the Landlord as the lover of notices. Certainly, the lady who delivered my lunch looked as though she had seen a ghost. She may have been his partner, leaving all speech to her pen-loving partner. There was something of the military in his bearing and manner. My every movement, after entering the hostelry, was dogged (sorry!) by a very corpulent canine. I think he was a Labrador prior to becoming a contender in the competition for a lookalike Mr Blobby. Little did this dog know how grateful I was of his presence.

Whilst waiting for my lunch, the journey caught up with me and I headed for the ladies where I was again greeted with yet more notices. These notices had been produced using a colour printer. If, on entering the ladies, you have a weak bladder and become waylaid and mesmerized by yet more notices then I hope you have a spare pair of pants with you. In the Landlord's defence, everywhere was scrupulously clean.

I returned to the bar to await my meal. I had ordered sausage, egg and chips. When the meal arrived, it all looked good, the egg had been fried as I would fry one at home. The chips were a generous portion and had some colour to them. Unfortunately, the three sausages had been lovingly marinated (overnight, from the strength of the taste) in Fairy Liquid. I sank my teeth into the first sausage and pondered whether its distinct soapy flavour was a Cornish delicacy. I do not dismiss new tastes out of hand. In Canada, some years ago, I had eaten baked beans cooked with maple syrup. My partner loved them but they were not for me. I decided to try another bite of sausage but had to discreetly remove this from my mouth using the napkin. What was I to do? The corpulent canine put out a paw and who am I to deny one of God's creatures some sustenance? The dog obviously wasn't averse to the flavour although I don't think they touched the sides as he wolfed them down. I decide to be philosophical about the lunch. After all, what can you expect for a fiver? Well, how about just one or two 'normal' sausages?

Note to the Landlord (only in black, I'm afraid). I apologise wholeheartedly if there are soapy bubbles emanating from your canine's nether regions. I'm afraid that if you keep serving these 'unusual sausages' then there is every chance that Fido will die of a heart attack aided by the noxious soapy substance.

FAREWELL TO MY FATHER—Christmas 2007

Before the scales fell from my eyes, you were arrogant, domineering, aggressive, dictatorial and always, always right. These traits were not imagined nor did they disappear but I came to understand that "the child is Father of the man".

When I was growing up I walked in fear of you. You sometimes "saved up" punishments until you had an audience. Once, when I was rude to my Mother you called me over and told me to hold out my hand. I was quaking with fear but you only tapped my hand lightly. I must have shown my relief/surprise and then came the real punishment. You told me to go straight to bed without putting any lights on. You knew I was frightened of the dark. Looking back and knowing you better, I think that every time you meted out an inappropriate punishment, you hurt yourself as well as me.

When you were frightened or emotionally upset you shouted. It was all you heard as a boy. What kind of a Mother tells you repeatedly that you were, and are, not wanted? You suffered violence at the hands of your alcoholic parents. One Christmas they bought you boxing gloves and a Mickey Mouse watch from a local market. Ma and Pa then went to their normal abode, the pub, and these presents were either left behind or stolen and you spent the Christmas with no presents. You became "the little boy that Santa Claus forgot".

When you broke your arm your Mother hit you all the way to the Bristol Royal Infirmary. I know that there was much in your childhood that you told no-one. It is true that I (among others) suffered because of your dysfunctional upbringing.

You had been in the Military Police during the war and you never forgot it. I never answered back; there would have been little point. However you told me that if I was in the Army I would be up on a charge of "dumb insolence". I guess my eyes "spoke" the words for me. You were wrong, in actual fact it was malice aforethought.

Even as a 'grown' woman you would speak sharply to me and suddenly I would revert to age four again. My head downcast, my eyes fearing to meet yours. My feet pointing inwards. Back then I would twist the hem of my dress with sweaty hands. I would pray for the interrogation to end. I wanted to shrink away to nothing but I could not escape your judgment. I didn't dare think outside the lines you painted. Most of the time I didn't dare think. The inner me absented myself from the tirade of how bad I was. I would try not to give you the satisfaction of knowing that you had "got to me". Of course I heard the words but I already knew I was not perfect—I was sent away to be mended. Strangely enough the various facial repairs I had did nothing to end the tirades. I guess I was just bad through and through. You were a highly critical parent. My Mother and I had an unholy alliance with regard to you. You must have been aware of it and for that I am sorry. When you are young you don't see the shades of grey just black and white. I cast you in the role of the merciless villain and my Mother as the ministering angel. How wrong I was!

You were always a "man's man". You were Chairman of the local Round Table and then the Rotary Club. You stood as an Independent candidate for the local Council. Behind the unforgiving Victorian façade stood a man who liked humour. You had a real penchant for telling jokes and I think I have inherited that. At the age of eleven I remember answering the door and you leapt out of the hedge, giving me a huge fright and then a fit of the giggles. You were dark and swarthy anyway, but had borrowed Mum's black eyebrow pencil. You parted your dark hair in the middle and plastered it with Brylcreme then blackened your eyebrows and moustache. You then put your jacket on backwards and crossed your eyes. No wonder I screamed so loudly. You directed and loved the Boxing Day parties we had. In 1962/3 we had heavy snow and during the night you built a huge snowman. It was over twelve feet tall and I still have the photo you took of me beside it.

You left in the year of my O levels with no explanation. You just didn't come home anymore. I was left with the nightmare that was my Mother and I resented that. I didn't miss your tyranny but I missed my Father. We were apart a long while and my Step-Mum tells me that when we next held each other she thought we would never let each other go.

You held very narrow views and condemned anything that was outside your comprehension. This could be foreign food, duplicity or being gay. I telephoned once to say I had a problem. Your reply was "are you going out with Martina Navratilova?" Me "no". You "then you haven't got a problem". But you were a great problem solver and I appreciated that.

In 1994, in one of my attention seeking moments I went missing and my husband called the Police. They wanted to know where I might go and so they got your address and telephone number. I made it home the next day and you rang and then ranted. Tears were pouring down my face and your tirade didn't need any reply from me. I desperately needed support but shouting was all I got. It was what I had come to expect from you and I decided I had had enough and said to my family that it would be a long time before I spoke to you again.

I think it was about two years until my step-Mum rang to tell me that you were terminally ill. I didn't hesitate and travelled up the next day. It was a bitter-sweet reunion and when you enfolded me in your arms I felt I had come home at last. How I wish that I could experience that embrace again. We are never satisfied are we?

You were told that you had eighteen months left on earth but, in fact, the cancer spread to your liver and you only lived four of those months. You never burdened anyone else with your despair and fear. I was and am just so proud to have had you as a Dad.

You went into the Hospice for less than a day and we drove as fast as we could to see you one last time. The call to come to the Hospice came at around 3 am. The nurse who let us in told us that you had passed away. Walking down the corridor, I silently prayed. "Please God help me to face another dead body". I wasn't sure that I could handle it but I had to try.

We sat around your bed and indeed you did look asleep. I will always remember your beautiful hands, strong, capable hands. You were pale but at peace with your arms resting on the white bedclothes. We sat with you drinking tea and at any moment I expected you to wake and say "where's mine?" We returned to the Hospice the next day to pick up your belongings, your watch and 51 pence. They had moved you to the chapel—you were still in a bed but changes had taken place and I stayed in the room for only a couple of seconds. As my Step—Mother and I left, I commented on the nice touch of the fresh white flower on your pillow. She then said that you hated white flowers and we laughed all the way out and I know how much that would have pleased you.

Time was marching on but you were time warped. You ended there and I began. I began a recovery time. I undertook a journey to consolidate the shards of my life—a last chance to be happy which is what you wished for me. I left you there in bed and went to continue my journey. I went to rejoin the frantic dance of life and you had just got off at the terminus.

Are you around somewhere, over my shoulder, above my head, watching and still caring for me? If you were here now I would lay my head on your chest and listen to the beating of your heart. How I hope we meet again.

"If two people who love each other let a single instant wedge itself between them, it grows—it becomes a month, a year, a century; it becomes too late."—Jean Giraudoux (56)

I cannot thank my Step-Mum enough for making sure it was not too late for my Father and me.

CATS—8 January 2008

"Dogs have masters, cats have staff" Anon (57)

The bus suddenly stopped in Wordsworth Drive. We had just gone over the speed bumps so they couldn't be blamed. On several occasions in the past, a driver has had to make an emergency stop because some youngsters kicked a ball into the road and then, unwisely, followed it. I couldn't see any children around but still the bus remained stationary.

The driver revved the engine to no avail. He then told us there was a cat curled up in the middle of the road. As a cat lover, I decided to stand up and watch the antics. More revving obviously annoyed the cat. The look in the cat's eyes said "How very dare you, **I AM A CAT**, I was here first, take a detour". The driver flashed his lights and the cat shot him another look which said "I ain't bovvered". It was stalemate and the cat wasn't going to give in. Eventually, someone emerged from a house and picked up the triumphant feline. The person looked decidedly sheepish so I expect that was the person the cat owned.

I have been owned by eight cats during my life and I am fully aware of the honour bestowed upon me by their ownership. Anyone who thinks they own a cat knows little of them. But they will learn. We know that little people (children) invoke tantrums and histrionics to get their own way, so you should expect nothing less from the cat who owns you.

Once the said feline allows you to share its home there is the question of food. You try various brands until you find the one the cat likes. He/she will consume the food like there's no tomorrow for maybe four or five days. The next day the cat gives you a filthy look which says "I'm not eating that rubbish". The plate remains full; the cat remains empty and leaves via the cat flap without a backward glance. Confused? You should be. Just when you thought you had sussed the feline out he draws the winning card and deprives you of his presence.

The lady at the end of our terrace has two indoor cats, one of which is deaf. I suspect my neighbour would describe herself as an animal lover. Unfortunately, she is torturing both cats by leaving food out for our feathered friends. How awful to have temptation that close yet so far away. I suspect that both felines will need psychiatric counselling and treatment for stomach ulcers brought about by the over-production of gastric juices. Wasn't it Billy Fury who sang "you take me halfway to paradise, so near but so far away"? Spare a thought for these troubled moggies.

My present owner, Tilly Trotter, never hesitates to let me know who is boss. She even managed to make me feel guilty for leaving her for 37 hours each week. The fact that I had to attend a place of work in order to buy the rejected cat food matters to her, not one bit. If I go on holiday, she will sit with her back to me on my return. I try my best to cajole her and make her feel special. When I have done my allotted spell of solitary confinement she will graciously allow me one stroke of her downy head. This is coupled with a look that says "Don't ever do that again". I remain in awe of her.

In the past year, TT has been mother, father and best friend to me. She often senses when I am down and she and I have shared some very bleak moments. Last January, when I made a very unwise choice of man, she rejected his strokes and viewed him from afar. Jealousy I hear you say—very likely.

From the day TT decided to own me she has been a scrupulously clean cat. There has never been an accident. Whilst "the unwise choice" was strolling down to the local shop to get a Sunday paper, I decided to read the Saturday paper that he had left in the floor. There in the middle of "his" paper was a cat turd. I hastily got rid of the incriminating evidence. On his return, I ask if he had finished with the paper and he confirmed he had, but asked why. I told him what TT had done and said that it might be a mitigating circumstance if TT had been taken short, but, from the evidence on the newspaper, she had not.

Later that month the "unwise choice" left without repaying me for a long haul holiday we had enjoyed. This cost me £800. TT was spot on with her statement—she has never deposited since and I frequently leave papers on the floor. She is a wise cat and worth so much more to me than gold or diamonds. In the evenings we snuggle up in my reclining chair and I am honoured that she lets me stroke her head and the purrs that result from this are magical and deafening!

On tonight's news was an item that caught my attention. The police had bugged a pensioner's home as they were convinced that he had murdered his partner. They got the evidence they needed when he said to his cat "they know that I did it". Priceless.

"Dogs come when called. Cats take a message and get back to you later". Mary Bly (58)

GETTING HOUSED—20 January 2008

I didn't have a clue about Housing Associations but decided to pick up the 'phone and find out more. Old neighbours had sold their house and were now living in a Council flat. When I say old I mean I'd known them a long time. They said they had been on the waiting list for five years. I picked up an application form for council flats from Taunton Deane but as I am not in receipt of any of the benefits listed I do not hold out much hope.

I have just accepted early severance from my job and although I will be able to survive for a while without working, the future beyond the end of that money is very unsure.

Writing a book speaks of a rusty typewriter and existing in a garret somewhere with only a candle and no heating. There's not much money to be made from writing unless your name is J K Rowling. I believe that she also was not flush with money when she wrote the first Harry Potter book. Can I box clever, cut the mustard, and put my money where my mouth is? What was it that Clint Eastwood said in the film "Dirty Harry"? "You got to ask yourself one question "do I feel lucky? Well do you (punk)?" All I know is I have to write this book and take my luck where I can find it.

Back to the housing issue . . . . the lady at the Housing Association asked me if I had a social worker. Apparently most of their clients do. It became clear from our discussion that if I was a one legged, bisexual woman of colour with umpteen children I could have the key to a property today. The HA lady laughed with me about this but then said that, sadly, it was true.

The fact that I have worked full time for most of my adult life works against me. It seems that the dues I have paid are going to support some of the younger generation who decide not to work after leaving school. This will, of course, give them more time to procreate and guess what? Their offspring will also be brought up with the attitude that the world owes them a living. Sorry—I'll get off my soapbox now!

Did you hear the story about the woman who was asked to complete a form for child benefit? She said that she had six boys and had called them all Wayne. The civil servant helping her with the claim said "Well how does that work?" She said "it's simple; I just shout "Wayne your tea's ready" or "Wayne "its time for bed" and they know I mean all of them". The civil servant said "Yeah, but how do you call them if it's a matter concerning just one of them?" She said "Oh then I just shout his surname".

THE 1950/60'S written February 2008

"God gave us memories that we might have roses in December"—J M Barrie (59)

I remember years ago much better than what I did yesterday. I am told this is age which is the only thing I have plenty of. Looking back at that period of time brought a myriad of memories. Ruched bathing costumes with rubber swimming caps which distorted the sound of the sea and made it seem even more mysterious. Packets of Smith's crisps—no flavours but the dark blue twisted packet of salt. Quality control was less rigid then—you either got a bag with no salt or up to six in a single packet. Who remembers the liberty bodice which gave you anything but liberty—those horrible rubber buttons yuk! Rainbow coloured net petticoats which scratched your legs to bits.

Saturdays—The Grandstand sports programme which went on forever and during which I would be shushed at least ten times by my Father. The first episode of Dr Who. Dixon of Dock Green. Always roast beef on a Sunday, after "Two way Family

Favourites". Tea of jelly and evaporated milk or pineapple chunks. Supper at 9.00—just for my Father—of roast beef sandwiches and pickled onions. I also remember a programme called "the Brains Trust" which my Father insisted I watch, listen and learn. I can't remember if it was aired on a Sunday but I soon learnt to "tune out" when this was on.

I spent a good deal of time with my Aunt Phyll who was a statuesque woman with a ruddy complexion. I always remember her working hard and her willingness (or foolishness) to cope with feeding four or more people who didn't want to eat the same food.

Phyll was a darling. She was not eloquent of speech but her every deed confirmed her love for her fellow man. When I stayed with her, I was allowed to be me—what a luxury! When I was young and staying with her, she would wash me. Phyll believed that cleanliness was next to Godliness and she attacked with a fervour any penticostalist would have been proud of. The wooden draining board was where I sat and she washed. I think there were times when I felt I could take no more scrubbing. Her allies were heavy duty flannels and Lifebuoy soap. My knees would turn a vivid orange colour and I would secretly pray "please God don't let Auntie Phyll wash me anymore".

Phyll was enthusiastic when it came to scrubbing the floors of The Gardener's Arms public house and she applied the same criteria when it came to washing small, grubby children. She would get carried away with the cleaning task at hand (and sometimes that was me) and she would break into song. She was almost tone deaf and her rendition of "Lay down your Arms" was always followed by another layer of skin being removed. Her favourite song which, to this day, makes me feel sad was "I'll take you home again Kathleen" It was an Irish lament and I feel her very close to me when I occasionally hear it being sung.

I spent some summers there with my cousin Liz. We ate lemonade powder until our tongues were discoloured and sore. She and I would wind in and out of the Golden Rod plants. We collected fallen rose petals and added water to make scent. Scent that by the following day would stink and be abandoned by us. I don't think there were many fragrances around in the early '50s. My Mother had California Poppies which really honked. She also had a small dark blue bottle with a silver top called "Evening in Paris" I thought that this perfume was very sophisticated and smelled divine. I wonder how it would fare against the huge range of fragrances today.

GRANDFATHER'S COFFIN 2 March 2008

My Grandfather's coffin was made from "unpolished elm with brass furniture". He died at the age of 56 in the late 1930's, many years before I was born. He had a massive heart attack. The funeral write-up said he had not been attended by a Doctor but had been "in indifferent health for some time". It was a quick and kind death for a well respected man. It says that he was "highly valued by his firm". He had worked for the Company for over 20 years starting as a joiner and being promoted to general foreman in 1924. There were 59 floral tributes to him with messages such as "In affectionate remembrance of one of the best pals and workmates". His chief hobby was floriculture and "he attended the flowers in his greenhouse on the morning of his death". Although the funeral report says that he was "a genial man and popular with all who knew him", I think his children were well aware that he was head of the household.

He worshipped at Paul's Meeting Congregational Church and formerly belonged to the Paul Street Brotherhood. Grandfather was a member of the Loyal Order of Shepherds for 45 years having joined as a youth. My Grandparents voted Liberal all their lives. My Mother told me that his open coffin was in the front parlour if people wished to call to pay their respects. The parlour was dusted daily. It seemed in those days that death was treated as part of life. My Great Aunt Dorothea told me that when her father was dying workmen spread straw in the road so that the noise of the horses' hooves would not disturb the dying. We obviously had a little more respect then. Life is cheap today. We watch massacres on television while eating our tea.

If someone dies now they are whisked out of the house very quickly. In the United States and, increasingly, over here the dead are embalmed and then cosmetics applied. This is for the benefit of the living and there is a danger that you could end up looking better than you did when you were alive! What we do know is that none of us will cheat death. We come into this world with nothing and we leave the same way. There are no pockets in shrouds—death is a great leveller.

Taunton, in the late '30s, was such a different place. There were tea dances at Dellers. At the cinema you could see Tyrone Powers, W C Fields and Will Hay. Films were changed twice a week. You could buy a Hillman Minx for £100 and a Woolsey for £245 from Somerset Motors. For £265 you could purchase a Sunbeam Talbot from Dunn's Motors. Pears Soap cost 4 1/2d. If you were suffering from "holiday stomach" you could get Milk of Magnesia tablets, a tin would set you back 6d. In the Gazette, deaths were recorded under a column headed "passed on". There was a typhoid outbreak and there were three fatalities in Taunton.

Grandfather's offspring did a rota of jobs around the house and he would check to see if they had been done properly. My Mother remembered becoming anxious when he ran his finger along the dado rail and said "Em, whose job was it to dust the passage"? I don't ever remember my Mother talking about him very much but he commanded respect. He believed in discipline. No housework was done on a Sunday. The roast dinner was taken to the local bake-house to be cooked and picked up on their return from Church. Packs of playing cards were not allowed in the house. He once caught my Mother shaving under her arms and told her, disapprovingly, that "God put that there for a reason". She didn't dare to ask what the reason was!

FEMALE—29 March 2008

It seems that the less I use "me bits" the more maintenance they require. Old age does not come alone. I have just had an invitation to have another mammogram—oh joy!

I don't mean to be critical of the Great Engineer but it would have been handy if the "bits" could have been made detachable. You could then just drop them off for any maintenance they require and pick them up later as you do with cars.

I think I was about 10 when my Mother told me that a friend who had been absent from school that day, had "become a woman". This statement was then followed up by an explanation of periods and the like. Although I was tall and well developed for my age, I was 13 before I needed to concern myself with that. I think I had my first bra way before I had a period. Of course I didn't really need a bra then, but it was a status symbol and something that I had nagged my Mother for. How I wish I didn't need a bra today!

Having a bra and periods were landmarks for me and my friends. I remember, purposely, leaving a bra strap on show waiting for someone to comment and they did with the words "you've got a flag flying". What a daft thing to say but it was a standard comment along with "Charlie's dead" which meant you were showing your petticoat. No one seems to wear petticoats these days. I was very impatient for my periods to start and then couldn't wait for them to end.

The PMT I suffered from the age of 28 to the menopause was bad—especially for those around me. I would get tender breasts, water retention and was very, very moody. I would be unreasonable and I would listen to myself knowing that but still continuing to dish it out. As my ex-Husband would say "we all suffer from PMT"!

A colleague at work regaled me with the story of his young daughter who had come home from school saying that her best friend was not at school and it was something beginning with P that was wrong with her. My colleague and his wife decided that maybe this was the time to tell her about periods and the birds and the bees. This is not always an easy task for parents but they didn't shirk their duty and explained the lot. The next day she came home from school and said "it wasn't periods that was wrong with her it was 'pendicitis!"

From the age of 50 my nether bits kept having to be overhauled. I firstly had an abnormal smear test and was sent an appointment for the Colposcopy Clinic at the local hospital. I dreaded this and had a few sleepless nights imagining it. From the 1950's when they told you naff all about any procedure they have now gone into overdrive. They sent me a leaflet which left me in no doubt as to what they were going to do. They also advised me to bring a pair of socks in case my feet got cold. Well it began with "f" but it wasn't my feet that were my concern.

The actual procedure was less traumatic that I thought it would be. I watched, on screen, as they took a biopsy. About four hours later I felt as though I had been kicked in the lower abdomen. I then had to have a yearly test at the Clinic and was then told that I could have this at my Doctor's surgery. They were keeping an eye on the situation. The last time I went the Nurse told me that if I wanted to relax my cervix I should smile. I asked her if she had smiled throughout labour. I don't think it was my imagination, but she went very quiet after that.

Talking of women's bits, I heard two stories which were amusing. The first was a lady who had to go to the Family Planning Clinic. She went home from work, had a wash and a quick spray with a feminine deodorant. After the smear test the Nurse thanked her for making the effort. She wondered what had prompted such a remark. All was revealed when she opened her handbag, she had sprayed hair glitter instead of Femfresh.

The other story concerned a lady who had to undergo an internal examination at a hospital. She sat in the waiting room and realised she needed to spend a penny. She found the Ladies loo but then found there was no toilet paper. Undeterred, she dived to the bottom of her handbag and found a clean tissue. Once in the stirrups, the Doctor asked her if she minded some students watching the procedure. Throwing caution to the wind, she nodded. The Doctor then asked for some forceps. He muttered, for the benefit of the students "they get everywhere don't they"? He then proceeded to remove a green shield stamp.

I haven't had periods for four years now and its absolute heaven.

> "A lot of men think the larger a woman's breasts are the less intelligent she is. I don't think it works that way. I think it is the opposite. I think the larger a woman's breasts are the less intelligent the men become"— Anita Wise (60)

Did you hear about the gynaecologist who decorated his house? He did it all through the letterbox!

ADDICTIONS UNLIMITED—4 April 2008

That could certainly have been the Andrews' family trading name. My Father was addicted to complete control and utter obedience. My Mother drowned in her own self-pity 'helped' along the way with many prescription drugs and anything you could buy over the counter at Boots.

I have, and will probably continue to have addictions. I am an emotional eater and enjoy alcohol. Someone asked me recently what my tipple was and I said it was Stella Artois or white cider. Talk about stating the obvious, they said "That's strong stuff". Of course it is, if I wanted Tizer I would have bought bloody Tizer!

The image of the 60's was sex, drugs and rock and roll. I lost my virginity at 19 to the man I would go on to marry. It was the era of the pill and so-called "free love" but for whom? I was a wild child of that era but have never smoked cannabis or taken an illegal substance.

There were however, a lot of prescribed medicines. I still call my medical records 'War and Peace' but I think it was mainly war. My Doctors, throughout the years, have all inwardly groaned when I walked through their door. Some of them, the really brave ones that is, have made that groan audible! There is no drug that's strong enough, or any bottle deep enough to cure you when you are heart sore.

At times, I've traded one addiction for another. I discovered the shopping channel—QVC. Jewellery and rings in particular, became my thing. I realised my need to rein things in and decided that I would only buy a gemstone that I did not already have and I would only buy 1 carat or more. Debbie Greenwood, one of the presenters calls a large stone up to three carats 'a whopper' and over three carats 'a stonker'. So I sat feeling safe with the rules I had set and then suddenly, there it was a huge green quartz ring. It was, as in the case of any addiction, love at first sight. How could I break the rules? It was true I already had a green quartz ring which was a stonker . . . . however, that was set in gold and this was in silver. In no time at all I rang and purchased the adored article. One can always find an exception to the rule if you try hard enough.

I have recently had a get well soon card from QVC and it is rumoured that they now have a chance to re-stock their warehouse following my temporary abstinence. I think many people, men as well as women, indulge in "retail therapy". If this becomes an addiction then indeed you will need therapy but not of the retail sort! QVC, please don't worry I still love ya! You sell top quality goods and I am sure our partnership will continue!

Another of my addictions, years ago, was sorting out the problems of those around me. I would get involved and sometimes take the action that I thought they should take. The problems of friends are a wonderful distraction to stop you from dealing with your own stuff. You can only deal with your own problems.

I'm not sure that anyone is born alcoholic or bulimic but I do believe we select our weapons carefully. One of my weapons is food. I say is and not was but I can now recognise it and that helps. I would say that food is not my problem but I have used it as a solution. My emotional eating which seems to be in abeyance at the moment, involves me getting "sweetie rage". If I am upset or angry, I head for the 'pick and mix' at Woolworths. I trample any children who stand in my way. Don't get me wrong, I like children I just can't eat a whole one, they are SO full of calories and they need to be cooked thoroughly before consumption. Once I have paid for 'my treasure' I stuff as many as I can in my mouth and swallow. I don't think I ever taste them and, of course, they are never enough.

I am already familiarising myself with my next addiction. I have tripped over my stepper twice and I dust my exercise cycle at least once a month. The aim is to get fit, lose some more weight and enjoy! Because I am lazy, I have some doubt whether this addiction is going to be added to my list. I know this piece of writing is entertaining but any addiction which does you long-term physical, emotional or financial damage (or a combination of all three) has to be dealt with by the grown-up who is hiding behind the Inner Child.

Footnote: I decided to test my temporary resolve **not** to buy any more jewellery by watching one of my favourite fashion jewellery shows. I am immensely proud of myself, I didn't buy a thing. However, on my lap there was a full packet of Maltesers now half empty. Bugger!

> *"Excess **on occasion** is exhilarating. It prevents moderation from acquiring the deadening effect of a habit"—W. Somerset Maugham (61)*

DIANA—8 April 2008

We are 11 years on and I wonder if she will ever be allowed to rest in peace? The Inquest has only just begun and looks set to run and run. Will we ever know the whole truth? One thing's for sure, everyone remembers where they were when they heard the news.

I had been in my New Single Me Flat for two months and I left the radio on beside the bed. I was still finding singleness strange. The radio was the voice of another human somewhere in the night. My sleeping had been really bad but that night I had slept from 11.00 until 4.30. I awoke, delighted with the time—it had been my longest sleep for quite a while. Then, as I adjusted my eyes and my brain clicked in, I heard the sickest, unbelievable announcement. The Voice said that Diana, Princess of Wales had been killed in a car crash.

It took me a long while to understand what I was hearing. So very, very sad—how would we manage without the People's Princess? I wanted to ring someone but knew I couldn't at that early hour. My mind was desperately trying to assimilate the gross unfairness of her early death. Eventually I spoke to my daughter and ex-husband.

My friend Daphne gave me a lift to Church each Sunday and I got ready rather like an automaton. When her car pulled up she said "Don't say anything". Words would have been inadequate and we travelled to Church in silence. Our prayers and thoughts were with her beloved boys.

I think people just got through that week on auto-pilot and were dreading the funeral. I asked to borrow a television from the Old Matrimonial Home and joined the nation in grieving. The Royal family badly misjudged the grief of the general public. But, life goes on and I moved in 1998 to my one-bed house.

My relationship with He Who Will Never Be Forgotten had been up and down and we argued frequently. I don't think he found it easy being on my turf. It was a Saturday and his birthday had been earlier in the week. I got some top quality steak which I would serve with new potatoes and asparagus—his favourite meal, next to curry. He settled down to do his crossword and I took a break from the kitchen. There was an article in his paper about Princess Diana and he just erupted, saying "She was the good time that was had by all". I challenged him about Charles' affair with Camilla. He Who Would Never Be Forgotten was having none of this and said that he would leave if I persisted in defending her. I said nothing, I just pointed to the door. He left and I cooked the steaks and ate mine.

I knew he would get in touch but I was determined that I would not reward his bad behaviour. I froze his steak and ate it myself later the following week. He made contact and we resumed our relationship and he always referred to that day as "the day we argued about the Royal family". He couldn't have been more wrong. We argued because it is still acceptable for men to have affairs but unforgivable if women do.

> *"What's sauce for the goose is sauce for the gander."*
> Anon (62)

GRANDMA—15 APRIL 2008

> *"Emotional sickness is avoiding reality at any cost. Emotional health is facing reality at any cost"*—M. Scott Peck (63)

If you cut yourself, you clean the wound, have a tetanus jab and cover the area to wait for healing. Why don't we afford our emotional life the same care? I am convinced that problems talked about become so much easier to deal with. There was a lot of collusion in my family and the wounds festered and grew deeper,

Marigolds grew in Grandma's garden. They were as intense and lively as Grandma was quiet and unassuming. I lived with my Grandma and parents until we were given a Council house in the 1950's. Grandma visited often and always brought me a tube of Rolos and a cuddle.

I remember the night the bad news came, very vividly. It saw me and my Mother searching the streets in our vicinity for a neighbour, Mrs Northmore. She was doing a house to house collection for a Catholic charity. There was no talk from my Mother just many, many tears. I skipped along beside her asking every 30 seconds "What's wrong? Why are you crying?" There was no reply just more tears.

We found our neighbour and I went to spend the night with her and her family. It may have been more than one night—I was to grow accustomed to being "farmed out" when my Mother couldn't cope. My Grandma had drowned. I don't know who told me that but I suspect it wasn't my Mother. It is said that old sins cast long shadows. It is not for me to decide what is a sin but if there was one it was the sin of omission. It was to be forty years before I found the missing bits of the jigsaw. The family closed ranks and any talk of the river brought tears but Grandma was not discussed. Unspent emotions and fears grow in the darkness that they have been consigned to, and nothing goes away—distortion and paranoia can grow unabated. I decided, back in early 1997, to send for the Inquest papers to find out what I could of my Grandma's death.

22 May 1997—A large envelope arrives, from the County Coroner and I calmly open it There are various statements but one strikes me immediately. An Aunt, giving some background on Grandma's life, said that Grandma had told her that she had had 17 children but only 8 grew up. My eyes scan these official documents searching for "the truth". Having been a legal secretary for years I have read and typed many dark secrets. These dark secrets belonged to other people and they were not mine. However, when they are personal 'secrets' it is a very difficult to be dispassionate.

I discover that a cousin of mine was living with Grandma at that time because Grandma couldn't bear to be alone. I get to the description of her clothing and how and where her body was found. I remember the dress she was wearing—I go to pieces and my tears flow for this gentle, loving woman who I missed so much. I knew now why I feared deep, dark water. Having my hair washed had to be with me lying with my back on the draining board so that the water would not go on my face. I still insisted on this when I was way too big for the draining board. When I was young, the mere mention of a hair wash sent me running in the opposite direction. Only the threat of my Father being told brought me to heel.

It was my Father who went to identify my Grandma and the sight haunted him. I feel distraught and in need of someone to pray for me—someone who can form the words that I cannot. I have not been to Church for some time. My spiritual home is Halcon Baptist Church. I know they now have a new Minister and the Manse is at the bottom of the road I live in. I somehow feel drawn to wanting to meet this man and request his help. I didn't fancy walking down the road in the state I was in to introduce myself. I decide I will 'phone. I telephone the number for Silver Street Baptist Church and am given the name of Andy Wilson as being the new Minister for Halcon, together with his telephone number.

I dial the number and say "You don't know me, my name is Rosie . . . ." My voice trailed off as this man says "You are wrong; you live at the top of my road. You have a husband called . . . . and a daughter called . . . . We prayed for you last night at a meeting". He tells me that he is on his way and to put the kettle on. He brought some writing that he had done and left this with me. This man of God had known times of emptiness and desolation. We talk, I cry, he prays. Andy is amazed that I should ring him because he and others had prayed for us only last evening yet we had left the Church many years ago. On his way out he shakes in head in disbelief. I say "Why should you be amazed? You prayed for something and you got it. That's not really trusting God is it?" I managed a chuckle so that Andy knows that I am not telling him off. Andy tells me there is a letter on its way to us to say that our membership had never lapsed and that we were always welcome. You could call it coincidence but I shall always call it an answered prayer.

> *"There are more things wrought by prayer than this world dreams of"—Alfred, Lord Tennyson (64)*

GOODBYE GRANDMA—19 April 2008

Did you think we would love you less because you could no longer cope? Surely you had earned enough credits within the family during your life, more than enough, to let others do the caring. But perhaps they had and you couldn't cope with being less than 100 per cent.

You saw one or more of your family almost every morning and evening. You visited "your girls" for tea most evenings. Your family was close and caring. I am no Sherlock Holmes but something was desperately wrong. During the year you had suffered from depression and dreaded being alone. Your right arm had become very shaky. You had only recently started to wear glasses to read and sew. Your hearing was good.

Although you had had flu and bronchitis in past winters, you had never had a serious illness or been admitted to hospital. You had a real dread of hospitals. You became withdrawn and short tempered. Apparently, you could not bear to be kept waiting in shops. You went to see the Doctor who gave you a nerve tonic and some sleeping tablets.

On the day of your death you were meant to be having dinner with one of your daughters. You didn't go for dinner and at around 2.00 pm you were seen, by a lady looking out of her front room window, walking across an iron bridge and then towards the lock in the field. She stated "Once in the field she turned sharp right towards the water". Three young boys came into the field and a few minutes later you came back across the lock and iron bridge. I believe that you delayed your death so that young lives would not be lost or blighted and I thank you for that. If only you could have done that for your family.

You then walked slowly towards the town. You seemed agitated. The lady who observed you then got her bicycle and went into town. When this lady got home her Mother told her that they had just taken a body from the water. "On hearing this I immediately thought of the old lady as I thought that by her actions she had contemplated suicide and I went to the iron bridge. I was able to identify her as the woman that I'd seen earlier".

I know you must have been desperate but I sincerely hope that lady suffered no feelings of guilt or responsibility. She wasn't meant to stop you. We all have to be responsible for our own lives. But your actions that day you showed the next two generations how to behave like a victim. For many years you had been the Captain of the ship but you had grown old and couldn't cope as you did when you were younger. Others would have taken over the helm and given you some much needed rest. You were, are and will always be my beloved Grandma and oh how I missed you.

GOODBYE GRANDMA 2. 10 May 2008

I went to the Local Studies Library to look for details of your death and funeral. I am amazed how a word, a fragrance or an old photo can transport me faster than any jet plane to yesteryear.

Your death hit the front page. It put your age as being between 60 and 65 and said that your dark brown hair was just beginning to turn grey. You were in fact, 73 so your face did not betray your age. I scan the next edition on microfiche and came across the funeral report and this really moved me deeply. The first floral tribute was from my family. My name was not included. I was stunned, I know I was young but how could I have been missed out? I felt cheated. I carry on reading and suddenly there it is a separate floral tribute which read "to my dearest Gran, from your own little girl, Rosie". I was special to you and you were oh so special to me. The salt tears welled in my eyes as I felt the pain of losing you all over again. I was determined that those tears would not flow in an inappropriate place. There is a dignity in me that was never there in the spoilt, hurt child that was me for so long. You would be proud of me Gran—I am nearly "growed".

July 2008. It is a hot July day and I have brought some vibrant red flowers to the river. I go to Goodlands Gardens ready to say "thanks for the cuddles and Rolos Gran". I find a quiet spot and wait until no one is near before throwing the flowers into the river. What I didn't know was that below me were a family of ducks who I had, unwittingly, disturbed. Much noise ensued. I didn't realise that ducks could swear, so much for my quiet goodbye. I love you Gran and love never ends.

DOWNTOWN TESCO 18 May 2008

> *"The hardest years in life are those between 10 and 70"*
> *Helen Hayes (65)*

> *"There's no pleasure on earth that's worth sacrificing for the sake of an extra five years in the geriatric ward of the Sunset Old People's Home, Weston-super-Mare"—*
> *Horace Rumpole (66)*

It's 7.40 am on a Monday morning in the biscuit aisle of Tesco. In front of me is a couple I know who happen to be retired. We exchange greetings and some small talk before we resume our shopping. I go to Tesco at this time before starting work. When I reach the checkout the wife is nowhere to be seen and the husband is piling the groceries on the conveyor belt. He had chosen a "buy one get one free" but had only picked up one, so had to return to get his second item. He brought that back but by that time the checkout girl had taken the top off the egg carton and there was a broken one. The checkout operator rang her bell to summon help. My quick shop was taking longer than I thought. A young girl eventually came and then wandered to where the eggs were. She appeared to have two speeds, slow and stop. An unbroken box of eggs eventually arrives at the checkout. At long last, I was able to put my purchases on the conveyor belt and I then discovered that he had left his loyalty card behind. I shouted after him but he did not hear me and so I sprinted to return the card.

I was telling my daughter about this experience and said that I would never be in Tesco at that time of the morning once I retired. My daughter said I was missing the point and that I would eventually join them in what was, for them, almost a nocturnal event. My daughter was delighted to be able to tell me that once retired I would wake up early and rise quickly to greet the day. She said "They know that time is running out and that's why they have to cram so much into their day. You'll be doing it to before long". Well I've been retired a number of years now and have, so far, avoided this habit. Not hearing the alarm go off at 6 am is sheer bliss.

HOORAH HENRYS 19 May 2008

As defined in the concise Oxford dictionary as being "lively but ineffectual young upper class men".

Once again I was enjoying a break in Looe. Having been a bit of a globe-trotter in my younger days, Cornwall is my first choice. It's ideal; if you book ahead you get very reasonable rail fares. Your luggage arrives with you and there is no jet lag.

In roughly three hours I arrive at my hotel, unpack and go for a stroll. I will never divulge which hotel I stay at for two reasons.

The first being mine Host/Hostess have enough trade as it is and secondly I would be really pissed off if no room was available having been previously booked by a reader of mine.

It's always nice to "touch base" with jovial people that you've met before and the happy hour extends beyond an hour. Generally, there is talk in the bar of local people and events, the price of fish and such like.

However, there was entertainment laid on tonight which didn't cost the proprietors a penny. I didn't count them but I think there were four or five of them. They were not raucous but if they had been female I would have described them as "jolly hockey sticks" or "OK yah". They spoke with a plum in their mouths. I heard one of them being addressed as Rupert and the whole evening I had to fight the temptation to ask him where his check trousers and scarf were. He kept referring to his "dahhling wife". I was sorry when they left but could just imagine Rupert arriving home to his dahhling wife and whispering "One would love to give one one dahhling".

LESBIAN—July 2008

I was in a bit of a dilemma. I have a real penchant for country music and am a fan of a duo that doesn't play in town much anymore. I met one of the boys in the Building Society and he told me that they were playing at a certain hostelry in town. The hostelry in question is what I would describe as "different". Some of the people who frequent it are dysfunctional. It's the sort of place where someone might say "So my girlfriend is my Mother, do you have a problem with that?" I think the Americans might describe it as being populated by "trailer trash".

So how much did I want to hear them play? Well enough to venture in to the hostelry. I decided to look resolute and I didn't glance from left or right. With my head held high, I ordered my drink and sat down. "The boys" were, as always, excellent and were pleased to see me.

Part way through the evening some people were dancing and suddenly a chap behind me asked me if I would like to dance. I declined politely and said that I had just come to hear the music. He wasn't easily put off as he said "Well other people are dancing and I noticed that you came in on your own". I countered with "If a man walked in here on his own would you go over and comment on it?" He was honest and said "no". Once again, he asked me to dance. I thought that I would need to be brutal and said "I'm old enough to be your Mother". He countered with "Well I'm 45, how old are you?" I said "I'm not about to tell you that but trust me, although it would have been illegal, I am just about old enough to be your Mother".

He decided to give up on his quest to get me dancing. The rest of the evening was excellent and my enjoyment of the music was heightened by the addition of two pints of Stella Artois. I stood up to leave and was again confronted by Taunton's answer to Dirty Dancing. He said "I've worked you out; you're a lesbian aren't you?" I burst out laughing, obviously he thought he was such a catch that I had to be gay if I didn't fancy him. I hated to burst his bubble but I told him that I was definitely heterosexual. I chuckled all the way home.

PANIC ATTACKS—27 August 2008

> *"Confidence is that quiet, assured feeling, just before you fall flat on your face" Anon (67)*

I had another one on Saturday. You would think that I would be an expert on them now but because they disappear sometimes for a year or more, they always catch me unawares. They have been part of my life for about 40 years.

I can't remember the first one or what occasioned it. I can, however, remember that in the 70's I worked as a secretary to a Solicitor and I was frequently called upon to witness someone's will. One day a client was staring intently at me as I signed my name and my handwriting turned into that of an old and frail person. I shook from head to foot and it took nearly an hour before I was "myself" again. After that, each time I witnessed a will I would turn into a quivering wreck.

You always think you are the only person who feels this way, but when I did eventually tell a Counsellor he said that it was quite common for people not to like being watched whilst they wrote. I shed many tears over what I thought was a permanent problem. Mr Seymour Blake, the first Solicitor I worked for was happy for me to take the Will to a little side table and sign it there. When a will is witnessed you have to be in the presence of the person signing and the other witness.

Eventually I moved back to Taunton and became a legal secretary in Hammet Street. My boss obviously saw what happened to me when I witnessed a document and was not in any way sympathetic. He said that he would always call on me as a witness so that I could "get over it". He was an excellent solicitor but had lousy 'people skills'. Each time that I knew that a client was coming in, I would hide in the ladies loo so that others had to do the job. I would get told off for doing it but I preferred the bollocking than the shame of the shakes.

The panic attacks did, however, save me loads of money. My favourite shop for clothes at that time was BHS and I lost count of the times that I selected a dress and queued up to pay. As I waited, so the tremors would start and I would eventually put the dress back as I was aware that my signature on the cheque would look totally unlike my 'normal' signature. I guess the 'up' side of my 'problem' was that I would never be bankrupt!

Panic attacks can be because of too little space (and I have experienced that) but for me mainly because there is too much space. As I said, I had an attack on Saturday. I live near a busy road and had to cross it to get to the bus stop. I waited until it was safe but my legs wouldn't move. I felt the panic rise within me as I knew the bus was soon due. I wandered further along the grass verge talking firmly and positively to myself. I'm a great one for looking at the worst possible outcome and if you can deal with that then the panic will subside. The worst that could happen to me in not being able to cross the road to catch the bus was that I would have to walk into town. A fair walk but it would do me good. I then managed to cross the road as calmly as I could.

Not long after I moved to my one-bed house, I decided that I could put up with my bedroom décor not one moment longer and so I headed for the DIY store. This meant taking a short cut across Victoria Playing Fields. I stood rooted to the spot knowing that I could not stride out across such a vast space. I could have cried but what good would that do? Instead I hit on the idea of walking along side the hedge. Anyone watching would have been quite entertained. The bottom line was that I didn't give in to the Inner Child and run home sobbing. It was a successful, if unusual day. I got my paint and I had to walk a little further—so what?

I can remember once going to visit an Uncle who had been unwell and a panic attack occurred, I was frozen to the spot, unable to advance or retreat. I spoke to the Inner Child and decided that humming a song would be a good distraction and so I did and it was. It was only at the end of my visit that I realized the song which motivated me and got me moving was "Keep right on to the end of the road". Panic attacks remind me of the giant cigarette in the 'give up smoking' advertisement. They loom large and even though I am their Master, because I know how they work and I manage the situation, I don't like them—not one bit.

> *"Courage is the art of being the only one who knows you're scared to death"*—Earl Wilson (68)

> *"The secret of success—fall down seven times; stand up eight"*—popular Japanese proverb (69)

AGE—30 August 2008.

"The idea is to die young as late as possible"—Ashley Montagu (70)

I know that I am (getting) old. When the leaflets first started coming through the door I would throw them away as something I didn't need. You know the sort of leaflet I mean, the ones that deal with nasal hair, trusses and bunions. I now scan them fervently, delighted when they advertise an aid that I don't need . . . . yet. Am I foolish to read them or just bowing to the inevitable?

I visit the chemist more than I did 20 years ago. Then the visit would have been to buy make-up. This week I visited the pharmacy counter. It was just my luck that I got male sales assistant. I smiled thinly and said that I wanted some haemorrhoid relief cream. "Pardon?" he said, moving slightly forward to catch my words. "Haemorrhoid cream" I said, upset that I had to repeat my request. He stared at me as if I were speaking Hungarian. I drew myself up to my full height and said in a louder voice "cream for the relief of piles". Was it my imagination or had the whole shop gone quiet, waiting to hear my request? I paid up and left with my head slightly bowed thinking "should I now go the whole hog and get a pair of tartan zip-up slippers?"

"Age is something that doesn't matter, unless you are a cheese"—Billie Burke (71)

BOOTS THE CHEMIST OCTOBER 2012

I persuade myself that armed with the name of the product; I would not feel so embarrassed in Boots. The ointment, for the treatment of piles, is called Anusol. I guess there's no disguising where that's going to go. I head to the pharmacy counter feeling fairly confident. I get another male member of staff who is older and looked more mature than the one who served me in 2008. I ask, calmly, for a tube of Anusol and then he asked me if I wanted a large or small tube. I just could not help it; I turned so that I was looking over my shoulder and said, with glee, "Well does my bum look big in this?" We both hooted with laughter and I left the store feeling pretty good. Laughter is, after all, the best medicine.

A couple of businessmen were fixing shelves in an otherwise empty shop and one says to the other "Some noisy old so and so will press their face to the glass and ask us what we are selling". Sure enough, a little old lady stopped and asked what they were selling. "A..holes" said one of them and the little old lady wisely said "Well, you are doing well, you've only got two left."

Why are haemorrhoids called haemorrhoids instead of assteroids?

Two men were asked by the Police to attend the morgue to see if they could identify a body. The body had been badly burnt and the Police warned them that it was not a pretty sight. Patrick goes in first and looks at the body, The Police ask "Is that Aiden O'Reilly?" Patrick asks for the body to be turned over and he looks the cadaver up and down and then says "No, that's definitely not Aiden." Shaun is then taken to view the body and the Police ask "Is this the body of Aiden O'Reilly?" Shaun also asks for the body to be turned over and, like Patrick, he then looks it up and down and says "No, it's definitely not Aiden". As the two are about to leave the Police ask them why they wanted the body turned over and how they knew it wasn't Aiden O'Reilly. Shaun tells them "Well every time we went out drinking with him people would say "There goes Aiden with the two a..holes".

LISTEN—10 September 2008

Who is there in all the world who listens to us? Here I am—this is me in my nakedness, with my wounds, my secret grief, my despair, my betrayal, my pain which I can't express, my terror, my abandonment. Oh listen to me for a day, an hour, a moment, lest

I expire in my terrible wilderness, my lonely silence. Oh God is there no one to listen?—Seneca (72)

God gave us two ears and only one mouth, so I think he is trying to tell us that listening is twice as important as speaking. Plenty of people think they listen well, few accomplish it.

To actively listen:

> Listen with your ears to what words are being said.
> Listen with your mind and heart to what is behind the words.
> Listen to what is **not** being said.
> Listen to silences—often these tell you most of all.
> Listen with your eyes—body language can be in complete contradiction to the actual words.
> Listen to yourself and your reactions to the person talking to you. Do you understand what they say?
> Listen—do not judge.

> *"His thoughts were slow*
> *His words were few, and never formed to glisten*
> *But he was a joy to all his friends*
> *You should have heard him listen."* Anon (73)

JAM—20 September 2008

> *"The rule is, jam tomorrow and jam yesterday—but never jam today".* Lewis Carroll (74)

He Who Will Never Be Forgotten often quoted this saying or rather his abridged version of it. He bemoaned the fact that there was "never jam today". I'm ashamed to say that I never actually knew where the saying came from and me of the literary ilk! There is also another saying that "tomorrow never comes".

So, it would seem that you have the choice to wait until tomorrow and hope you make it through, or to have jam today. Admittedly, it might not be the strawberry jam you had hoped for. Maybe you will have to settle for apricot jam but there is jam and you can enjoy it now. We all need rewards, even little ones. If you put your life on hold in your quest for top quality jam you may well be disappointed with the taste after waiting so long and you may have no one to savour it with.

Whilst on the subject of food, Shirley Conran said "Life's too short to stuff a mushroom". If you are a cook (and I am) and/ or a connoisseur of mushrooms, you may not agree with this statement. But there is nothing to stop you agreeing with the idea behind it. We busy ourselves with the minutiae of life; we get immersed and sidetracked until it is too late. We've been so busy attending to boring details that we miss the beauty of the whole picture.

IT'S DIFFERENT NOW—21 September 2008

"Fear is a little dark room where negatives develop"—
Michael Pritchard (75)

Late in 2006 I started to lose blood—not a lot, but it was a sign that something was amiss. I went to my Doctor who referred me to the hospital. Although not a member of BUPA I belong to a scheme which pays for the first consultation and could get an early appointment. My Doctor assured me that I would be seen within two weeks through the NHS. In fact, it was within 10 days—incredible. I took it as a good sign that my cat shared the surname of the Doctor.

I had a biopsy taken and attended as an outpatient to have the polyp removed. I was given some local anaesthetic as the Consultant entered my womb and attempted to remove the 'alien'. The nurse squeezed my arm, almost conspiratorially, and said "it's not much worse than bad period pain is it"? I think she needed reassuring. I didn't reply as I thought a fist in her gob might upset her. The consultant then decided that, as it was a large, fleshy, 'alien', I might bleed to death and render a consulting room unusable for the rest of the day.

The words I had always dreaded left his lips and assaulted my ears. "You will need to come in and have a general anaesthetic" he said. The death knell rang in my head and I knew there was no escape. I was sent for a pre-operative assessment, something new to me. There were pages of questions about your general health, medications, past operations, anxiety level and even "have you ever smoked cannabis"?

There was a space on the form to be filled in by the nurse concerning your height and weight. I was in for no surprises there; I already knew that I was too short for my weight. I eyed up all the nurses that were milling around and hoped that I would get the fat one. Even if I didn't I decided that it was fruitless to get into a discussion about my weight as I could never lose the amount that I needed to within a fortnight.

Under the heading of allergies I wanted to write "general anaesthetic". As a child I had been held down and the mask forced over my face. A necessary evil maybe, but I never forgot it. It was obviously my lucky day as I got the fat nurse. She weighed me without comment and I made a mental note to kiss her feet on the way out

She asked me why I was anxious about the operation and I was given ample time to explain about past experiences. I explained that the actual operation didn't bother me at all. I was terrified by loss of control, plunging into the black abyss, the fear of never being conscious again. She told me that, provided there was no one whose medical need took priority, I would be the first down for surgery after lunch and I didn't need to arrive until noon. I explained about my denture and the fact that I cannot eat, drink or speak (intelligibly) without it. Again she noted this and said, that depending on the anaesthetist, I might be allowed to retain it for the operation. I had never been so well treated as I was that day.

In the past I had always been "the patient", the one whose face was drawn on by surgeons. These men looked at the flesh but failed to see the person behind it. I know that you need to be somewhat dispassionate, but there were many times when I was just a heap of flesh. That kind of treatment scars you on the inside.

The day eventually dawned for the operation and I think I was probably more resigned than terrified. The 'alien' had to be removed and I had to be unconscious. Nurse Helen Chasemore asked if I would like her to walk me down to theatre. I got on the couch but then had to adjust myself so that some of the ties on the back of the gown could be undone. Helen assured me that no one would see me completely without my gown. As far as I was concerned, if one leg was in Devon and the other was in Somerset, it didn't bother me. The staff could invite their friends and have a party once I was unconscious.

Helen held my hand as "I went under". It was gentle and not frightening. I guess you could say that I grew up at that moment. In recovery I was asked about my pain level and was immediately given drugs intravenously. Years ago, you knew that after coming round from the operation you were going to have some pain. I never recall having any pills or injections for pain. The only time I had any further drugs was when my throat became infected and I had to have a course of antibiotic injections in my rump and they did hurt. I don't think it was the actual injection but the 'heaviness' of the fluid. I have always been extremely lucky that I have never thrown up after surgery but some patients did and still do. What a come down from the elation of knowing you are still alive and then the experience of projectile vomiting. Welcome back to planet Earth!

BEING DIFFERENT—26 September 2008

"It's not that easy being green
Having to spend each day the colour of the leaves
When I think it could be nicer being red or yellow or gold
Or something much more colourful like that"
—Kermit the Frog (76)

Different (according to the Concise Oxford Dictionary) 1. Not the same as another or each other; unlike in nature, form or quality. 2. Novel and unusual. 3. Distinct; separate.

Normal (according etc) conforming to a standard; usual; typical or expected.

Because things are different today, I am going into Musgrove Park Hospital for a further (and hopefully final) operation on my nose. This will be my tenth operation. The fear of being "put out" remains with me but the Adult can calm my Child sufficiently to let this operation happen, at least I hope so.

(Three days later). We are such complex characters—the diversion tactics I've employed rather than write this piece are amazing. Why don't I want to write it? I guess it's because I'm not 'normal'. I rang Blake Ward yesterday to find out if a family member could stay with me whilst I'm being put out. I got the ward administrator who doubted that this could happen but said to check with the nursing staff. I felt ok but when I finished the call I realized I had tears in my eyes. The thought of the forthcoming operation makes me vulnerable hence the tears—not such a grown-up bunny after all.

All my life I've wanted to be normal. Plain Jane would have been fine—fading into the background would have suited me. I'm no saint; we all take a second look when we see something 'not normal'. I've seen Simon Weston twice, once driving through Taunton in the early morning and once walking with his wife in Cardiff. Because of his burns he is so distinctive.

After getting some photographs from Frenchay Hospital, I sent for my notes. My first admission was on 1 January 1951. I was discharged, after two operations, on 23 February 1951. It was a long time to be without my Mother's arms. The operation was carried out by Mr Bodenham. I remember him well, he was tall with thinning hair but the thing I remember the most was his gentleness and kindness to my Mother and me.

The other plastic surgeon involved in my early reconstruction was Mr Fitzgibbon. I'm sure he was an excellent surgeon but his people skills were rubbish and neither my Mother nor I liked him. He was of the opinion that children should be seen and not heard. I'd like to think that he would have read his own children a bedtime story but I think he would have judged himself 'above' that. Do you know the difference between God and a doctor, God knows he's not a doctor. All joking apart, I thank God for Mr Fitzgibbons' skills.

Ward 30 in the '50's and '60's was run like a communist regime. You could bring sweets and chocolates which had to be handed in to share among all the patients. You were allowed one sweet a day which was directly after taking the dreaded spoonful of iron medicine. This really hacked me off as I would take the medicine, eat the sweet and within two minutes throw up. Taking the medicine was judged as being "good for you". In my opinion it just made more work for the staff as the loos were at the end of a corridor and even though I ran I didn't always make the loo. Maybe they should have positioned me in the loo before giving me the medicine or—really, really radical—not give me the bloody stuff in the first place!

After being admitted, my Mother and I would put my washing gear into my locker. It was done in silence by me whilst my Mother tried to sound enthusiastic about my new flannel and soap. You could bring a toy with you from home but it had to be sterilized in the autoclave. My bear, Teddy Edward, would not have liked that treatment so no comfort from him.

Sister encouraged parents to leave as soon as possible and I would watch my parents walk back to normality. My Mother would stop every two steps to wave to me and it felt like a stab in the heart. I had become aware that my parents were no longer the ultimate authority. This now belonged to the nurses and surgeons. Within an hour of being admitted I was visited by the most beautiful vampire I had ever seen. She fixed you with her vibrantly blue eyes then pricked your thumb and drew the resulting blood up using a suction tube. I remember thinking that such a beautiful creature could surely have got a nicer job!

The first morning would see you being given a general check-up and then the photographs. I never ate on the first day of admittance—the sights around you were just too much. By the third day you were conditioned and I was able to eat while someone next to me was throwing up. Obviously, I shielded my plate while this was happening, I didn't want any extra portions!

In preparation for the Surgeons' rounds, Sister and the nurses became visibly twitchy. All hospital corners on the sheets were inspected and all pillowcase openings had to face away from the door. You sat upright on a chair by your bed. I remember once trying to sneak a look at my notes and photos and boy did I get a bollocking from Sister. It was only the documentation of part of my life after all!

You were not allowed to lie on or in your bed during the day unless it was medically approved or was your 'operation day'. The surgeons came and played this game. It was called "let's talk over her head and draw on her face". In 1962 I can remember two young surgeons arguing as to whether they should do both the lip and the nose together. Unfortunately, the wrong surgeon won and both were done. Because there was loads of gunk coming away from my nose the lip never healed properly. I had to have the wound sprayed with some noxious substance that took your breath away in order for it to heal.

There was a school at Frenchay which you had to attend on week days providing you were well enough. There was one teacher to deal with a vast age range. I didn't like him—he was one of my captors—he lived in the outside world and was allowed to return there each evening.

Something that I always found strange was Matron doing her rounds at midnight. She shone her torch in your face. Whether she had to do a head count I don't know but when you opened your eyes because of the brightness she would tell you to go to sleep. I just smiled and forgave her. She was as round as she was high with eyes that twinkled like the stars. She didn't need a torch the beam from her face was enough. She looked as though a cuddle would not have been out of the question if she was asked.

I remember being 12 having had my pre-med injection and watching the ward clock. I strained my ears, dreading the sound of the wheels of the trolley as they came to take me into the blackness. I never ceased to marvel at the kids who had this jab and were asleep when the theatre assistants came to take them to the theatre. Many of these kids were first timers and ignorance is bliss. I never slept once and the fear grew as the ward clock ticked. I was always convinced that once the fluid was pumped into the back of my hand, I would cease to be.

Visiting for me was on a Saturday or Sunday and it lasted two hours. My parents relied on the train and bus service. Both my parents worked and cars were a luxury in the 1950's. There was no such thing as 'special leave' or being welcomed to stay with your child at that time.

On Sunday mornings we had a rare treat. Two very enthusiastic young men came with a portable organ. We were their heaven on earth as we were a captive audience with nowhere to go and nothing better to do. One of the choruses they taught us was "I will make you fishers of men" and I thought this was spelt FISSURES because of the state of all of us.

You may be thinking that this is all negative but that was because of the way I perceived it. My life has been made easier by each operation and I am very grateful for that.

BEING DIFFERENT 2. 1976—28 September 2008

"Be careful what you wish for—you just might get it" (77)

In 1976, whilst I was masquerading as an adult, I was offered some life-changing surgery. My husband and I attended Frenchay Hospital to prepare for this. Believe me, whatever I went through so did he—and some! He was incredibly patient and kind—he knew how much it meant to me.

The mandible (lower jaw) was to be shortened by a quarter of an inch each side. This necessitated the removal of my wisdom teeth which was sad as they were in good condition. I had a gum problem and had to have a gingevectomy.

Six months after the mandible healed, the second operation would follow. This involved bringing the maxilla (upper jaw) forward and remodelling the nose and the lip. It would be ten hours on the table. Each time I visited Frenchay they would ask me to try and eat more. My jaws would be wired up for some considerable time. I was a size 10 and despite a diet including beer and pizza I could not put on weight. Now I can't seem to lose it! Each time I saw the oral surgeon's Registrar I emphasized that I was taking an MAOI drug for depression. I knew there were contra-indications with a drug of this sort.

The operation was set for 11 October, just before my birthday. I left work on the Friday and my colleagues said goodbye to the old me. Foolishly, I thought that if I looked right then I would be right. I got home to find a telegram which I still have. I guess it must have meant a lot to me. It says "Operation cancelled—please telephone Frenchay".

You can't have a general anaesthetic with an MAOI drug. It was made clear that I would need to come off the tablets before surgery could happen. So, stupidly, I stopped taking them without weaning myself first. I plunged into a very deep depression and then I caught measles and was really poorly. Within seven months I was an inpatient at the local Mental Hospital. My mood was one of bitterness and regret. Although these operations would have transformed me physically, the mess on the inside would remain the same. I had no emotional intelligence at that time so I thought that surgery would remodel the whole me. I seethed inwardly and outwardly. The mantra of "poor me, poor me" went on and on and I bored people to death with it.

I saw specialists again in 1997 and was told that I could still go ahead with the surgery—I wasn't interested, the time had come and gone. There is an entry in my hospital notes dated 24 September 1976 which says "Opinion—if anyone is going to get deterioration from osteotomy this woman should!"—the exclamation mark was included in the notes. Nowadays, any disadvantage of surgery has to be explained prior to treatment. Back in 1976 surgeons/doctors were under no such obligation. I asked for an explanation and was told that although my looks would certainly have been better, my speech could well have been unintelligible. But, it could have been improved with yet another operation! My friends know that I've got a gob on me and communication is something just so vital to me. Not to be understood would have crushed me. I really do thank God for denying me these operations.

> *"I have had prayers answered—most strangely so sometimes—but I think our heavenly Father's loving kindness has been even more evident in what He has refused me"—Lewis Carroll (82)*

BEING DIFFERENT 3—1 October 2008

The surgery on 20/10/08 is very much to the forefront of my mind. I had a dream a couple of nights ago and was horrified to hear a young surgeon waxing lyrical on the surgery he had performed on the roof of my mouth. He had not touched the shape of the nose at all. Luckily, my surgeon is not young and will do the best he is able to with my nose. He has already told me that I will not have a small nose which is right—I don't have a small face.

Having had many previous plastic surgery operations I'm realistic as to what can be achieved. I don't expect to be a lookalike Audrey Hepburn. She was stunning—was being the correct tense as she's no longer with us, so I really don't want to look like her! I will settle for a smaller nose. I had to sign a form warning me of infection and also there is a chance (according to the surgeon) that I will not like what he has done and want further surgery. If the nose is smaller then it's fine, I don't see me becoming addicted to surgery. I shall be grateful for small mercies. I may lose a piece of cartilage from my ear as they (those long-ago surgeons) may have taken too much away when the last operation was done. I'm never satisfied—the possible need to use part of my ear was a piece of information I could have used post-operation!

The playground was not a pleasant place for me and I still suffer with low self-esteem. I even went out with a chap in my teens who wouldn't kiss me because of the scar on my lip. I didn't complain 'cos I felt I wouldn't kiss me either. I also have a female relative who makes sure she avoids my lip when we greet each other.

At the present time, I have hearing loss and a deficient sense of smell which may decrease further. I also face loss of taste—that could be a good thing if it stops me eating all the 'bad' things. Orthodontics is an ongoing process for me. I have thickening of the sinuses which may require surgery at some point. The clarity of my speech may also deteriorate with age. Certainly, when I am tired or have a cold then my speech suffers. BUT I am an extremely lucky bunny. I have two arms and legs. I have been loved and have loved in return. I have the most amazingly talented and beautiful daughter.

I'm really hoping that this book sells and sells well—it's not just me who is depending upon it. I am donating £1 from each book to The Smile Train which is a registered charity. The train travels to foreign climes and operates on children who have a cleft lip and/or palate and if you see the 'before' and 'after' photos you will know that this transforms lives. Many parents in the poorer countries put their disfigured child into state homes with no hope of an education and/or surgery.

I guess it's being comfortable in your own skin. Kermit puts it much better than I can.

> *"When green is all there is to be*
> *It could make you wonder why*
> *But why wonder, why wonder*
> *I am green, and it'll do fine*
> *It's beautiful, and I think it's what I want to be"*
> —*Kermit the frog (79)*

BUT HOW DIFFERENT IS DIFFERENT? 2 October 2008

> *"The human spirit is stronger than anything that can happen to it". C C Scott. (80)*

My 'different' nose and lip are nothing to the suffering I have seen others go through. One girl, who was about seven years old when I met her in Frenchay Hospital in the 1960's, was burnt from head to foot. She had been left to babysit her brothers and sisters and a paraffin heater overturned and caught her dressing gown on fire. Her burns were so extensive, her face just a mass of burned flesh. She didn't speak and had a tracheotomy to aid her breathing. When she had had enough of life she would remove the tube and all hell was let loose until it was found again. I think it was her way of putting two fingers up to the world. She remained in hospital for very long periods to have umpteen operations. The nurses gave her a birthday party—but she didn't even get a birthday card from her family. I feel anger on her behalf and I'm sure she felt it deep within herself.

A boy was admitted on Guy Fawkes Night. His friends had thrown him on the bonfire—he was in absolute agony. I also remember a very angelic good looking boy with gorgeous curls. He had been involved in a road traffic accident and had to have his heel stitched back on. After several days the whole ward was filled with a sickening stench—gangrene had set in and further surgery followed.

MONDAY 20 October 2008

I am shaking from head to foot. Foolishly, I thought I had beaten my old feelings about losing control, as my operation last year did not cause me much distress. But, of course, this is an operation on my face and the terror is still within me. The one positive effect is that it works wonders on the bowels!

I catch the two buses necessary for me to get to the Hospital and immediately meet a woman with attitude. It was 11.20 and I was due to check in at noon. This obviously upset the receptionist as she challenged me for being early, stating that the bed would not be ready. I had to fight for control but calmly managed to tell her that I had to get two buses to get there, so I had the choice of being early or late. I had a book with me and I was happy to sit in the waiting area for as long as it took.

At noon I was taken to my bed and a nurse showed me where the gents and ladies loos were. I was told that I could use either as they both had locks. The nurse also pointed out the exit, which was temptingly close. For a few seconds I looked at my coat on the end of the bed and then at the exit. A voice in my head was screaming "Run for the hills, go now". Luckily, the adult in me made a convincing plea—"the theatre is booked, the surgeon is here and you asked for this operation".

When the Anaesthetist came to check on me I admitted my terror and asking for a pre-med. As I was staying in over night he was happy to prescribe 10mg of Temazepam. He also said I would be going to the theatre in about twenty minutes. There was no time to waste, so when the nurse brought the pill and some water, I hastily crunched it up and then swigged some water. The nurse's face was a picture and she asked what it tasted like. It was vile but I needed it to work ASAP.

I was given a slippery sheet to lie on as she said "You will be asleep when they come to collect you for theatre". I gave her a withering glance and said "No, trust me, I won't" and indeed I wasn't. As usual, I had been given a gown with the lower ties missing and I dreaded walking past the men's bay of the ward. Oh for a bum like Felicity Kendall in her hey-day—no make that now! I didn't need to worry about the gown they took me to theatre in a wheelchair. I don't remember the recovery room at all.

The next thing I knew I was back in my bed with a large bandage on my ear and feeling a little the worse for wear. I had a mini sanitary towel suspended under my nose and was given a straw to drink with. Each time I sucked on the straw my nose would drip blood. I was told that provided I was not still bleeding I could go home the next day. I managed to lift the sanitary towel and take little sips of luke-warm hot (?) chocolate. The drink was dispensed by a hot young male nurse who had his hair jelled and sticking up as is the fashion. I wondered if he used his own jel or used the stuff at the entrance to the ward and in the toilets. Even though the female toilet was further away, I used it every time simply because every woman who came out was rubbing in the gel and not one man came out doing the same.

I was given strong painkillers to take home with me which I didn't need. In Frenchay Hospital back in the'50s and '60s if you had complained about pain the attitude would have been "Pain? Well of course you have pain; you have just had an operation!"

If I could have a head transplant I would have the face of Vivien Leigh, the mind of Helen Keller and the emotional intelligence of Graham Stanier ("the genius" on Jeremy Kyle).

I am in the process of deciding whether to enter myself for the Turner Art prize. If an unmade bed with dirty underwear can win, why not me? It's not every person who has half their ear stuffed up their nose!

DOGS—Christmas 2008

I've decided this year to put my Christmas tree up and decorate the lounge. Last year I just could not be bothered. I guess it's where your head is, at the time. Goodness knows why I feel more optimistic this Christmas—maybe its hormones or something. I keep thinking that 2009 has to be better so the decorations will confirm my hope for the future.

I've noticed other people's decorations and they do not please me. On my way to the Doctors, I pass at least three bags of dog excrement hanging from trees and hedges. Does someone raid the bins that are available and then 'decorate' these trees and hedges? Even more bizarre, is the option that people have taken their dogs out with the little plastic bag and collected up the faeces only to throw them heavenward. Is the message "Yes, I'm a responsible pet owner." followed by "But not in my backyard". It's a crazy world out there!

FALLING APART—2 March 2009

> *"Acknowledge that everyone, at least once in their life, will lose it; be overwhelmed with negative emotion, speechless or incoherent. They will fall apart"—Rosie*

These are some of the rules an Adult would follow:-

You must **NOT**:-

Bleat—it's a terrible noise coming from a sheep and singularly unattractive if it emanates from a human being.

Fall apart during work time. (I plead guilty to this several times!).

Shout or scream (except when in your own company and preferable when the neighbours are out).

Embarrass other people.

It is possible to delay the physical falling apart until a later and more suitable time and place (this comes with age and plenty of practice).

It is acceptable to fall apart in front of a friend, not an acquaintance but a true friend. One who knows that you can, and will, return the favour.

It is important to let emotion out but it is unattractive spread across the front page of your local newspaper. In the main, people will remember the inappropriate behaviour and not the reason behind it. Even if supplied with the reason they may still not understand. What will incense one person may leave another unperturbed.

Falling apart on public transport or in someone else's house (except the true friend's) is unacceptable. Falling apart in the full blown sense is not allowed in your own home if you are entertaining friends.

If you feel the cracks appearing then gird your loins with some emotional blue tac until you are safely alone.

DON'T JUDGE A BOOK—10 April 2009

"The Lord sees not as man sees; man looks on the outward appearance, but the Lord looks on the heart"
The Bible (81)

We have done it yet again. The last time it happened an overweight man in an ill-fitting suit, who didn't smile, shuffled onto the stage. No one sighed with longing or expectation. He was asked why he was there and he said that people said he sounded like Pavarotti. Loud titters of laughter came from the audience, he sang and the rest is history. His name is Paul Potts and I know that his life has changed immeasurably since that time. I'm also quite sure that he is still self effacing and modest.

Recently, a lady who looked older than her years also took her place on a stage. She wore dark tights with a gold brocade dress. Her hair looked like the perm had grown out some time ago. None of this mattered when her voiced wowed the audience and me. People were on their feet and she went from being the laughed at underdog to the doyenne of the moment with many more moments to come. Her voice was just so beautiful and I have watched too many times to count, to be, once more, lifted by her singing. I have wept at the purity of her voice.

We are such fickle creatures, we assume good looks mean a good person and vice versa. The sad thing is that we will continue to do this. Even though we see "different" people featured on television, we stare and point and comment. I used to be an arctophile (a collector of teddy bears) and always picked the bears that had a wonky arm or eyes that weren't quite right. I knew what that felt like so I was determined to give them a home. I became their Rescuer.

There is one man who particularly stood out as being "different" and today we can't even get his name right. He was known as the Elephant Man and was called Joseph Carey Merrick. He is frequently called, incorrectly, John Merrick. Today we know that he suffered from neurofibromatosis or Proteus syndrome but unfortunately that knowledge would do little to stop our curiosity.

His unsightly tumours started to develop when he was just two. His Mother, Mary Jane, who was also physically handicapped, died when he was eleven. A new step Mother made his Father choose between her and Joseph. He lived for a while at the Leicester Union Workhouse. His life was full of cruel taunts and he could have become a very bitter and angry person. He made his living as a circus freak and at one point had £200 which was almost a fortune at that time. Needless to say he became a target for robbers and was tricked by another showman out of all of his money.

He was found at Liverpool station by Dr Frederick Treves and ended up living at Whitechapel Hospital. He became famous and was visited by the upper class of London. He went on outings but was still studied, naked by medical students and endured humiliating examinations. He was softly spoken and intelligent and he died in his sleep on 11 April 1890. He had tried to lie down to sleep as a "normal person". The weight of the tumours on his head asphyxiated him. I think I can do no better than leave the final words on this subject that was attributed to Joseph.

> *"Tis true my form is something odd*
> *But blaming me is blaming God*
> *Could I create myself anew*
> *I would not fail in pleasing you.*
> *If I could reach from pole to pole*
> *Or grasp the ocean with a span*
> *I would be measured by the soul*
> *The mind's the standard of the man"* (82)

HEP IS NOT HIP—22 April 2009

"Apprehension, waiting, expectation, uncertainty, fear of surprise do a patient more harm than any exertion"—Florence Nightingale (83)

Nightmares are bad enough but when you are enduring a living nightmare the world becomes a crazy place and you a crazy person. I had to telephone to get the results of my blood test and the automated voice told me that there was a problem. I had to wait from Thursday evening to Tuesday morning to be able to speak to a Health Advisor. According to the card I had been given they were only available on Tuesday, Wednesday and Thursday mornings between 9 and 10.

Knowing there was a problem and having to wait was not a good feeling. Little did I know that my nightmare was just beginning. After three attempts I managed to get a human being on the other end of the telephone. This pleasant sounding lady told me that I had tested positive with Hepatitis C. She then started asking me such bizarre questions. She started with "do you share needles with anyone?" I just could not believe what I was hearing and had to remind myself that this person did not know me. My reply of "No, I've never even smoked cannabis" was followed with yet more bizarre questions. "Do you have tattoos? Do you have body piercings? Have you had a relationship with anyone of Asian extraction? Have you ever had a blood transfusion? Being tattoo-less with just my ears pierced and no Asian boyfriends, I was struggling to comprehend the diagnosis I had been given. Hepatitis C is acquired by blood to blood contact.

I was told that I would need to have another blood test as they sometimes have a false positive result. I presented myself for the second test and again the questions came. I could feel myself getting angry when the needle sharing question came up again. It is true that I did knit two sweaters in the 1970's but I bought both the No. 10 and No. 8 needles myself and didn't share them.

After having the test I did say that I had had a lot of surgery to which there was no reply. I was asked if I would like to have some counselling, I declined. I had to waiting another 10 working days for the result of the second test. In the meantime, I went from knowing nothing of Hepatitis C to becoming an expert on it. Of one thing I am sure, it's not a disease that you would wish on anyone. There is treatment which is unpleasant and given my propensity for depression, I made up my mind that I would not be having it. It was only partially successful with two of the strains of Hep C and had unpleasant side-effects.

Hep C can be stored in the body undetected for decades. It was not identified until April 1989 and there are an estimated 170 million people worldwide who are infected. Evel Knievel (stuntman), James Earl Ray (assassin of Dr Martin Luther King), Pamela Anderson (actress), Anita Roddick (Body Shop), Ken Kesey (author of One Flew Over the Cuckoo's Nest), Natalie Cole (daughter of Nat King Cole and also a singer), and David Crosby (Crosby, Stills and Nash) are some of the many sufferers.

Whilst waiting for the second result I made an appointment with my own doctor and ran through the various scenarios in which I could have become infected. She said she was 99.9% sure that I contracted Hep C through early blood products. No one's fault but a bit of a bummer.

I consume huge chunks of Hep C knowledge from the Internet and when I rang for the result I guess the angels must have been smiling. It confirmed that although I had had Hep C at some point in my life my own body had dealt with it. I asked if I would need check ups and whether I could pass it on to anyone else and was told no. My Hep C was an old infection which is no longer active. I decided I wanted that in writing and for the princely sum of £5 I picked up, the next day, a letter confirming this. I am indeed a very lucky individual!

A PORCINE PROBLEM—18 APRIL 2012

"The way to a man's heart attack is through his stomach"—Anon (84)

Once again, Cornwall has beckoned. I have returned for another holiday amidst people I have come to know as friends. There is amongst them a Jack the lad, a wheeler dealer, a bit of a Del Boy. On my first visit I met Tony in the Hotel bar. He was easy to talk to but slightly the worst for wear. He's fond of his own voice and that hasn't changed in the years I have known him. There have been times when his mouth has had trouble connecting with his brain. It seems the more he imbibes the more trouble he has getting his lips to form words, but he remains undeterred.

He is very like Toad of Toad Hall and there is something endearing about Toad. Part of you wants to hug him and the other part wants to slap him. The first time I met Tony he asked me for a kiss on leaving. I declined saying that he was someone I had just met. He asked me if I thought he was good looking and I told him that he was not my type. Since then we have been firm friends. He actually has a heart of gold but just never knows when to leave the premises. He has a beautiful daughter as have I, so we have things in common. He has traded in many commodities. It seems that his latest venture is . . . . pork, yes pork.

On Saturday afternoons he raids the supermarket for marked down meat and then sells on the joints (pork not cannabis). Because of his fondness for alcohol, it is not uncommon for him to have no idea what he has sold and to whom. One unsuspecting customer was about to get an added bonus. Tony is prescribed Viagra tablets and these, because he's a wheeler dealer, are sold on to gentlemen who need them.

Donna and Chris are a couple I have only just met. They have bought a cottage nearby and are in the process of modernising it. Donna bought a piece of pork and when she unpacked it she saw that it had cuddled up to the Viagra tablets. Chris, as is the way with men, made some comments about pork and stuffing. Donna usually accompanies pork with apple sauce. Not being Cornish by birth, Donna wondered if this was a local custom. But she was more concerned about getting the tablets back to Tony whilst being discreet and tactful. She need not have bothered. The locals were out on the verandah of the Hotel smoking and they sent up a chorus of "Have you got Tony's Viagra?" Half the town knew about the pills as Tony had spent the morning on the 'phone endeavouring to find out who his customers were and who had the added extra.

An elderly man went to the Doctor to ask for Viagra tablets. He had had a very regular and good sex life with his elderly wife and felt that Viagra would make things even better. The Doctor was loathe to prescribe the tablets given the man's age. However, the man insisted. The Doctor said that as it was obvious only a little help was needed the pensioner should take a pill, skip a day, take another pill, skip a day etc. A month later the Doctor sees the elderly wife in town and enquires after her husband. She told him he had died and the Doctor, feeling guilty, said that he should never have prescribed Viagra to which the wife replied "Oh no Doctor it wasn't the pills it was the skipping that killed him."

The chemist shop was robbed and Viagra tablets were stolen. The Police are looking for hardened criminals in the possession of swollen goods.

A man goes to the Doctors because he had been sunbathing too long and had got badly burnt. The Doctor writes him a prescription. Checking to see what the Doctor had prescribed, the man was surprised that he had prescribed calamine lotion and Viagra. The man queries the Viagra and the Doctor explains that it's to keep the sheets off of him at night!

A woman walked into a pharmacy and spoke to the male pharmacist.

She asked "Do you have Viagra?"

"Yes" he answered.

She asked "Does it work?"

"Yes" he answered.

"Can you get it over the counter?" she asked.

"Well, I can if I take two" he said!"

> *"A hard man is good to find!" Anon (85)*

COMMUNICATION—Spring 2012

> *"Any problem, big or small, within a family, always seems to start with bad communication. Someone isn't listening" Emma Thompson(86)*

> *"Communication—the human connection—is the key to personal and career success". Paul J Meyer (87)*

There is no doubt that men and women communicate in vastly different ways. A few years back I was travelling on the bus to work and talking to another lady who I only knew because of the journey we shared. Christmas was coming and as a stocking filler I said that I was going to buy some gel inserts for shoes for my daughter. She wears, as I did, when fashion was more important than foot health, ridiculously high heels. A voice from the back boomed out, "Superdrug have got them on offer—buy one get one free. I know because I work there".

On another early morning bus trip a few days later I bemoaned the fact that I had lost the telephone number of my mobile hairdresser as she had moved. Another voice said "I've got the 'phone number for Shellie Rowlands if that's who you mean" and it was indeed. Many women are keen to help lighten the burden of others, male as well as female—they are keen to share and most take delight in helping. It's almost part of our genetic make-up. It gives us a buzz to help. Many women share easily of their time and experience. We trade details and rejoice in being of one mind. BUT men and communication well, that's another matter.

An intelligent male I know had not had a holiday this year because the last puppy had not been sold. He had taken his dog for a walk whilst she was in season. He was careful, as he knew there were some farm dogs where they usually walked. He foolishly let her off the lead when he thought it was safe. Needless to say, when he called her, she did not return. He eventually found her being extremely familiar with a farm dog but he managed to get the dog off. I asked what his wife had said and he said that he hadn't mentioned it as he thought he had probably got away with it. The dog gradually started getting fat and family members commented on this. He was forced to admit what had happened. He thought that playing dumb would cause less hassle. Men seem to want the easy life which doesn't actually exist. They do not comprehend the fact that women will go mental when they eventually find out and we nearly always do. He told me that they were now getting the dog sterilised—I told him I was amazed that his wife had not booked him in for a similar procedure minus the anaesthetic.

A little girl asked her Mother if she could take the dog for a walk. Her Mother said "No, because the dog is in season". The girl went out to the garage and told her Father what her Mother had said and asked what it meant. Anxious to avoid an explanation, he poured some petrol over an already oily rag and then gave the dog's nether regions a good wipe. "Now you can take her for a walk" he said. Twenty minutes later the girl came back without the dog. Her Father asked where the dog was. The girl said "Well I think we ran out of petrol but its ok because another dog is pushing her home."

Two men spy each other in a pub. One says "Hiya mate, how are you doing?" Yeah good mate and you? Fine—what are you having? A pint—thanks". This, for a man, is an in depth conversation. He is not interested in the fact that the other guy's got brown shoes on with black trousers. Neither is he interested in whether the other guy's marriage is good or bad.

AGE—June 2012

I notice that my "senior moments" are happening far more frequently. We all have had times when you go upstairs to fetch something and then your mind goes blank. You stand upstairs, castigating yourself for having forgotten and knowing full well that the minute you hit the bottom step your memory will be miraculously restored. I also find that I get easily distracted.

Last week I cleaned my downstairs windows and stood back tired but proud of my effort. As I put away the Windolene clear spray, I noticed that it had turned into Asda's antibacterial spray. I am now safe in the knowledge that if anyone licks my windows they are not going to catch anything nasty.

Yesterday, after feeling guilty about the lack of housework and the impending threat of a visit by a house proud friend, I decided to attack the house rather like a whirlwind. I would also time myself as an incentive. I lost the whirlwind feeling in the bathroom. I climbed into the empty bath and started to dust some bottles on a high shelf. I had bought, from "that shopping channel", some SBC products (Simply Beautiful Cosmetics). There were three bath soaks matched with identical skin gels. In my hurry to mimic the whirlwind, I knocked one of these off the shelf and it landed on my bare toes. I decided that speed could have its drawbacks. As I bent down to rub my foot and retrieve the bottle, I notice its Arnica skin gel. I dispensed a good dollop of the gel onto my fingers and thence to my toes. Housework would have to be a more leisurely pursuit if I was to remain undamaged so I am thwarted once again.

"Age is a very high price to pay for maturity" Tom *Stoppard (88)*

"Age does not diminish the extreme disappointment of having a scoop of ice cream fall from the cone" Jim Fiebig (89)

DRESS SENSE—February 2013

It was truly horrific. I can't remember the last time I saw anything that bad. It was just short of a crime against humanity, certainly no one's spirit could be lifted with a dress like that on view. The girl was tall and slender—so unlike me—she didn't have to grab the only dress that would fit her from the rail in Evans. The colours were garish and the pattern randomly awful.

She seemed to be unaware of the effect her dress had on the rest of her fellow humans. If her parents had bought it for her, I wanted to tell her to divorce them (an American concept I think). She should, at the very least, leave home. Perhaps her boyfriend had bought it for her. If so, she should dump him straightaway, he's a loser. If he bought it AND told her she looked good in it then not only was he a loser, he was also probably playing away from home. Maybe the dress was his insurance that no one could possibly fancy her dressed in such an abomination.

As she got further away from me, I was struck by the thought that she may well have, in a moment of madness, bought it herself. Should I go after her and, if I did, what would I say? People generally don't like to heed good advice and so I just muttered to myself "It's amazing what you see when you haven't got a gun."

THE BEAUTIFUL GAME—5th April 2013

"O Jogo Bonito"—which means the beautiful game— Pele (90)

"They say football is a matter of life and death. Frankly, it's much more than that"—Bill Shankly (91)

I really don't know if my Father would have enjoyed being on Twitter. Given that he died in 1996, I think he would have thought that Twitter was a kind of bird food.

My Dad's professional playing days ended before I came on the scene. But he was never cured of his love for the game. In his earlier days he played for Bristol Rovers and Charlton Athletic. As his professional sports life waned, he played for Torquay United and Taunton Town. He managed Taunton Town for a while. Even at the end of his life he would spot someone with promise and ring a talent scout. When he was unable to play football to the standard he liked he took up cricket and golf. He played three holes of golf just five days before he died.

Anyway, back to Twitter. I am a member of the Feel Good Factory at my local gym. It's a women only club which uses toning tables. I don't know how the conversation came about but I said that my Dad had been a professional football player. Penny, who was on duty that day, asked which clubs he had played for and was very excited when I mentioned Charlton Athletic. Apparently, that's the Club her husband supports.

The following day I took a postcard dated 4 January 1945 to show her. It stated that he had been selected to play against Chelsea Reserves on 6 January 1945 and to be at the stadium at 2.15 pm. Penny took a photo of the postcard and was amazed that this was the means of communication. I explained to her that back in 1945 people didn't have their own 'phones. Anyway, she sent the photo to her husband who contacted the Club and hey presto Dad was on Twitter. Back came an e-mail containing details of my Dad who, back then, was 19 and weighed 13 and a half stone. I was able to fill in some blanks in their records and I felt a kind of misty blueness 'cos I miss him like hell.

When he played for Taunton Town my Mother washed the team's kit each week. She was paid 2 shillings and 6 pence which today equates to 12 and a half pence! The most my Dad was ever paid for playing in a match, even as a professional, was five guineas which equates to £5.25. The ball, when it became wet weighed a ton. The shorts were really quite long and my Dad would have decked any player who tried to hug or kiss him.

A teacher in a Manchester Junior School asked her pupils to put up their hands if they supported Manchester United. There was just one hand that didn't go up. The teacher said "Mary, I notice that you have not put your hand up, why is that?" Mary says in quite a firm, confident voice that her Dad supported Leeds United, her Mother supported Leeds United and she supported Leeds United. The teacher then asked "Mary, if your Father was a thief and your Mother was a prostitute what would that make you?" The ever confident Mary replies "A Manchester United fan Miss".

A man's idea of a romantic evening out? A candlelit football stadium.

It's the Cup Final and a man notices that the seat next to him is empty. He says to the man next to it, "I just can't understand why someone would pay for a seat and then not come to the match". The other chappie says "Well, actually, it's my Wife's seat. We always come to see the Cup Final, but she died". The first man feels guilty and says "Well, surely a member of your family or a friend could have come with you". "No", says the other guy "they are all at the funeral". Perhaps Bill Shankly was right after all!

URBAN MYTH—6 April 2013

An urban myth is an entertaining story or piece of information of uncertain origin that is circulated as though true. Oxford Concise Dictionary.

According to Lady Antonia Fraser, Marie Antoinette never actually said "let them eat cake". It was apparently said 100 years earlier by Marie-Therese, the wife of Louis XIV. There was also another error as the word "cake" is a mistranslation. In the original French the alleged quote reads "Qu'ils mangent de la brioche" which means literally, "let them eat rich, expensive, funny-shaped, yellow eggy buns"! Doesn't quite scan does it?

Urban myths breed freely and easily especially given an alcoholic drink or two. When one is about to be uttered it is often introduced with the words "many's the time" or "in my day". In the 1930s, 1940s and 1950s it seems that "a policeman's lot was not a happy one" (thank you Gilbert and Sullivan). They apparently spent a long time taking home errant youngsters (mainly male) who had been caught scrumping (stealing from an orchard or garden) apples. The youngster would already have been the subject of corporal punishment inflicted by the policeman and then dragged home by the ear only to receive a further slap from their ashamed parent(s). It's a wonder that more serious crime got dealt with at all!

And now another myth exposed . . . . Drum roll! According to wikianswers.com, Queen Victoria did not say "we are not amused". Her diaries were, however, filled with the saying "we were very much amused". Is nothing sacred anymore?

Don McLean wrote a song called "American Pie" and is quoted as follows:—"In a sense "American Pie" was a very despairing song, but it can also be seen as very hopeful. Because of an off-hand funny comment I made backstage at a concert years ago, a story circulated that the song had been a burden and even that I didn't sing it for a while. That's completely false. I am very proud of "American Pie" and the many satellites that grow from it and revolve around it. For many years I carried my songs around and now they carry me around. I have always sung "American Pie" for my audience and would never think of disappointing them since it is they who have given me a wonderful life and untold affection for almost 30 years. I have never said a bad thing about the song, I was poor when I wrote it, and it made me a millionaire overnight. Believe me; I'm not upset about this song." The urban myth that I heard was much more succinct and funnier. Apparently Don was asked what American Pie actually meant and he said "It means I never have to work again!". I prefer 'my' version.

I have, of course, saved the best till last. It is really doubtful that this scenario happened but, once again, it is very entertaining. "When Apollo Mission astronaut Neil Armstrong first walked on the moon, he not only gave his famous "one small step for man, one giant leap for mankind" statement but followed it by several remarks, usual communication traffic between him, the other astronauts and Mission Control. Just before he re-entered the lander, however, he made this remark "Good luck, Mr Gorsky".

Many people at NASA thought it was a casual remark concerning some rival Soviet Cosmonaut. However, upon checking, there was no Gorsky in either the Russian or American space programmes. Over the years, many people questioned Armstrong as to what the "Good luck Mr Gorsky" statement meant, but Armstrong always just smiled.

On 5 July 1995 in Tampa Bay, Florida, while answering questions following a speech, a reporter brought up the 26 year old question to Armstrong. This time he finally responded. Mr Gorsky had finally died and so Neil Armstrong felt he could answer the question.

When he was a kid, he was playing baseball with a friend in the backyard. His friend hit a fly ball, which landed in the front of his neighbours' bedroom windows. His neighbours were Mr and Mrs Gorsky. As he leaned down to pick up the ball, young Armstrong heard Mrs Gorsky shouting at Mr Gorsky. "Oral sex! You want oral sex?! You'll get oral sex the day the kid next door walks on the moon!"

PICKING UP THE PIECES—8 May 2013

> *"Your feelings are so important to write down, to capture and to remember because today you are heartbroken but tomorrow you will be in love again"—Taylor Swift (92)*

The end of your first love affair is probably the hardest of all. No-one enjoys pain and, if you have been betrayed by a partner, there is anger too. I remember taking a young friend who was heartbroken, to see the film "Notting Hill" and she sat sobbing at one point of the movie because that particular song had been played to her by the man who had betrayed her.

So often when we see our friends and relatives in such emotional pain we want to wade in and try to be some form of anaesthetic. All we can do is to be there. We know, through experience, that there has to be a healing time and how long that is depends on the depth of hurt and anger and hopefully there will be some reflection on what went wrong. We can't circumnavigate the hurt; we just have to go through it. Recovery will happen if we allow it to.

I was recently talking to a very presentable man in his early 70s who had never married and I asked him why he had not looked for a relationship earlier in life. His answer was "Well, I got hurt". I like and respect him but I had to say "well haven't we all". No one is going to come and knock on your door and beg you to stop being a recluse—your life, in that respect, is in your hands.

I think that, as you get older, every love song reminds you of some one. I've said to my daughter "Go out there and make several men very unhappy. I've taught you all I know".

IF ONLY YOU REALISED . . . . 24 May 2013

"Vanity is my favourite sin."—Al Pacino (93)

"Vanity can easily overtake wisdom. It usually overtakes common sense."—Julian Casablancas (94)

Many years ago, when I was young and slim, I was amazed at my Husband's forbearance. We were at a New Year's Eve party and one of the hosts held me in a close embrace as we smooched together. It did not seem to faze my husband who was watching. He had a knowledgeable, self-assured smile on his face. At the end of the dance he told me, with much relish, that my long, black velvet skirt was tucked into my knickers. It is quite correct that he, who laughs last, laughs longest!

Fate conspires somehow to take us back to reality. I remember an evening (I was no longer married) when I felt hot to trot. I'd had my hair done, applied my make-up carefully, selected a becoming outfit and was, in my opinion, looking good. I can remember standing up to dance and my roll on, rolled off and instead of slimming my stomach it just made it more prominent. I managed to get to the ladies and remove the offending garment. I enjoyed the music and the evening. It was only when I arrived home that I could see that I had a piece of broccoli stuck in one of my front teeth and there was more mascara on my cheeks than was on my lashes.

One Saturday evening, again when I was looking good and feeling confident, I went to hear some music at The Westgate Inn. Paul Blamey was, among other things, a barman there. I had finished my outfit with a crochet short sleeved top. Paul told me that I looked good and said that his Mother had a similar one. I thanked him and preened my feathers. He then said that his Mother kept her sprouts in hers!

REVENGE—28 May 2013

"Revenge is a dish best served cold"—Pierre Ambroise
François Choderios de La Clos (95)

Revenge is sweet and not fattening"—Alfred Hitchcock (96)

*"He broke her heart. She broke his X Box. I think we all
know who cried the most"*—Anon (97)

I have just taken another antihistamine tablet. The tree pollen
count must be high today. The box warns me that the tablets
may make me drowsy. I hope this won't affect my typing. Alcohol,
before it makes me drowsy, badly affects my typing. It makes all
the keys on my laptop re-locate and eventually the screen also
goes fuzzy. Funny that!

Before I write this piece on revenge, I need to tell you that I did
think about leaving out the "Taffy" saga from the book. I think
the reason for this was my gullibility. But I did gain a cracking
piece of writing from it and my revenge was served cold. In fact,
I waited five months before my revenge came into force. I would
love to tell you what I did but I would have to kill you afterwards.
Seriously, if I meet you face-to-face, I'll be happy to tell you.
Enough!

So how do we get revenge? A young colleague cleaned her
toilet with her former partner's toothbrush before handing over
his belongings.

I also heard of another lady, who was asked for the return of
the photo her ex had given her. She borrowed from friends
and colleagues and sent fifty odd photos in an envelope. The
message said "I can't even remember who you are, so take your
photo and post back the rest!" I was also drawn to the story of a
jilted woman who gained access to the house of the man who had
married another and gone off on honeymoon. She and a friend
stitched prawns into the hem of the lounge curtains. Nice one!!

My friend, Donna, is a peaceable character. She had never broken the law before. She is kind to the elderly and nice to young children. She has impeccable good manners. She is just not the sort of person to be involved in breaking the law. But break something she did. She had reached the end of her tether when she realised that Chris was seeing another woman. She fumed and fretted. She paced up and down her lounge like a lioness. It must be said that alcohol did play a large part in the scenario that followed. She went to Chris's house and broke a window and then went home. In no time, the Police were knocking on her door. Donna admitted straightaway what she had done and was carted off to spend the night in a police cell. I've no doubt that she felt as though she were living through some kind of nightmare. She was given a caution and she paid Chris for the cost of replacing the glass. He, by that time, realised that he had chosen unwisely, they kissed, made up and have been together ever since.

> "Heaven has no rage, like love to hatred turned,
> Nor Hell a fury, like a woman scorned"—Congreve(98)

> "People think that I must be a very strange person. This is not correct. I have the heart of a young boy. It is in a glass jar on my desk." Stephen King (99)

> "At my lemonade stand I used to give the first glass away free and charge five dollars for the second glass. The refill contained the antidote." Emo Phillips (100)

DEMELZA—5 June 2013

Some people never learn do they? Chris and Donna seemed to be rock solid. Well, they were until SHE came along.

I can't say when the relationship started, but it is clear that Chris is besotted with her. He has even met her parents and you don't do that if it's not a serious relationship. Demelza is young, attractive and intelligent. She is definitely flirty and has a shapely pair of legs. I had always been told that if you wanted to know what your girlfriend would look like in later life, then you should look at her Mother. This does not bold well for Demelza. Her Mother looks a bit frayed round the edges and has a gammy leg. Chris just doesn't seem to care.

Does he not worry about the windows in the house? Imagine the premium on the insurance if they all had to be replaced. Poor Donna, she now has another contender for Chris's affection. Even when they go shopping Demelza is still on his mind as he is always on the lookout for tempting treats for the shameless hussy. And what of Donna who has always been a one-man woman? Has she resigned herself to the fact that Chris has extracurricular needs?

Actually there's no need to worry about Donna. She is still a feisty woman who has no trouble in expressing her feelings. Chris prefers her to do this in the garden away from all that tempting glass. I am having a cup of tea with them tomorrow and I'm expecting Demelza to put in an appearance. By the way, Demelza is a seagull.

AMAZONIAN RAIN FOREST—July 2013

"Grey hair is God's graffiti"—Bill Cosby (101)

Even though I wear trousers, I feel I could not go to the Feel Good Factory with legs that look like the Amazonian rain forest. I have shaved them and feel, marginally, more confident. I have started to wonder about the hair on my body. It seems that some is being re-routed. The hair on my legs, which can be seen by others, remains dark and plentiful. I can almost feel the start of its regrowth when I have put the razor away. My undercarriage is viewed by no one except my Doctor and only then when strictly necessary. So what the hell has happened there? I have sprouted hair on my big toes and the upper lip has also become a hirsute area. Is someone having a laugh? I am a great fan of the film Dr Jekyll and Mr Hyde starring the late Spencer Tracy. It's an old black and white movie but has some stunning shots of Dr Jekyll's smooth skinned hands turning gradually into the hairy maulers of Mr Hyde. I find myself staring at the back of my hands and waiting for the transformation. It doesn't last long as my degree of Alzheimers takes over and I forget what I am staring at them for.

> *"What's wrong with you men? Would hair stop growing on your chest if you asked directions somewhere?"—Erme Bombeck (102)*

"Why did Moses wander for 40 years in the wilderness? He was a man and wouldn't ask for directions."

WHAT MEN NEED TO KNOW ABOUT WOMEN —July 2013

Peach is a colour as well as being a fruit.

Placing a hand in an intimate place after just having a humdinger of an argument will not make us happy. Ever!

We always find out in the end, so save time and energy and be honest now.

We bought you socks with the days on, not to remind of the day, but in the vain hope you would change your socks daily. When you do eventually change them, they should be together in the laundry basket. Hunt the sock really p.sses us off.

Farting loudly or silently is not a prelude to sex.

Sex is not more exciting when you have guests staying over. It is non-existent. This also applies when we stay over at someone else's house. Do not try to shorten any holidays because of this.

There are items in the bathroom that are not for use. They happen to compliment the décor. Touch them and you are dead! Do not feel safe using items of a differing colour, they may well be there to provide a contrast in colour. Don't risk a miserable week check with Attila the Hen first.

We won't always tell you when the rules change—we like the element of surprise.

HOUSEWORK—3 August 2013

"Housework can't kill you but why take a chance."
Phyllis Diller (103)

"My theory on housework is, if the item doesn't multiply, smell, catch fire or block the refrigerator door, let it be. No one else cares. Why should you?"—Erma Bombeck (104)

I visit a lady who will be 91 in September. She has raised seven children. She has also cooked and cared for many people who seem to come to her door. No animal was ever turned away if they needed food or comfort. One cat, and there were many over the years, brought her kittens in and tucked them in beside the fire. Needless to say, they were looked after. When the children were small "Mum" worked, as a dinner lady and her husband had several jobs to ensure the family had what they needed. Not what they wanted, but what they needed. One Christmas morning he was in bed when the children got up to discover that Father Christmas hadn't been. He suggested that they look in the bathroom. They had a separate toilet and Dad knew that none of them would stop for a wash before opening presents!

"Mum's" hot water tap takes half an hour to fill a washing up bowl. When I commented on it she said "Well, I'm not going anywhere am I?" She still has a keen sense of humour and a plaque which says "I don't mind you looking at the dust but please don't write in it." She is a joy to be with and if she spent all her time doing housework I would be much poorer in spirit because of that. She is a beautiful person who has time for others and is always "fine" if you ask how she is. To take a quote from a country song that I love "She stood in the shadows so others might shine, she loved a lot in her time." I am just so grateful that she came into my life.

My friend Lorraine, to whom I have co-dedicated this book, loves housework. Luckily she has many other redeeming qualities so I can forgive her this quirk in her character. She would never put housework in the way of a visit to or from a friend.

I know many men today help out with the housework. I don't have a partner but my cat and I had a 50-50 split which is only fair. She would put the fur down and I would pick it up. Lucky me!

A woman was sitting at a bar enjoying an after work cocktail with her girlfriends when Steven, a tall, exceptionally handsome, extremely sexy, middle-aged man entered. He was so striking that the woman could not take her eyes off him. This seasoned yet playful heart throb noticed her overly attentive stare and walked directly toward her. Before she could offer her apologies for staring so rudely, he leaned over and whispered to her, "I'll do anything, absolutely anything, that you want me to do, no matter how kinky, for £20.00 on one condition". Flabbergasted but intrigued, the woman asked what the condition was. The man replied, "You have to tell me what you want me to do in just three words". The woman considered his proposition for a moment, and then slowly removed a £20 note from her purse, which she pressed into the man's hand along with her address. She looked deeply and passionately into his eyes, barely concealing her anticipation and excitement, and slowly and meaningfully said . . . . "Clean my house."

> *"At worst, a house unkempt cannot be so distressing as a life unlived."* Rose Macaulay (105)

Printed in Great Britain
by Amazon

17485921R00098